Financial Reporting Rules

and Corporate Decisions:

A Study of Public Policy

**CONTEMPORARY STUDIES IN
ECONOMIC AND FINANCIAL ANALYSIS, VOLUME 36**

Editors: Professor Edward I. Altman and Ingo Walter, Associate Dean
Graduate School of Business Administration, New York University

CONTEMPORARY STUDIES IN
ECONOMIC AND FINANCIAL ANALYSIS

An International Series of Monographs

Series Editors: **Edward I. Altman and Ingo Walter**
Graduate School of Business Administration, New York University

"To Our Wives"

Financial Reporting Rules and Corporate Decisions:

A Study of Public Policy

by BERTRAND HORWITZ
School of Management
State University of New York
at Binghamton

RICHARD KOLODNY
College of Business and
Management
University of Maryland

Ai JAI PRESS INC.

Greenwich, Connecticut   *London, England*

R 65887

Library of Congress Cataloging in Publication Data

Horwitz, Bertrand, 1927–
   Financial reporting rules and corporate decisions.

   (Contemporary studies in economic and financial
analysis; v. 36)
   Bibliography: p.
   Includes index.
   1. Corporations—United States—Accounting.
2. Trade regulation—United States.   I. Kolodny,
Richard.   II. Title.   III. Series.

HF5686.C7H67   658.4′03   81-81651
ISBN 0-89232-230-6   AACR2

Copyright © 1982 JAI PRESS INC.
36 Sherwood Place
Greenwich, Connecticut 06830

JAI PRESS INC.
3 Henrietta Street
London WC2E 8LU
England

ISBN NUMBER: 0-89232-230-6

Library of Congress Catalog Card Number 81-81651

Manufactured in the United States of America

CONTENTS

List of Figures

List of Tables

Preface

In the *Report of the Advisory Committee on Corporate Disclosure to the Securities and Exchange Commission,* Professor William Beaver raised a fundamental question. Why, he asked, was it desirable to have a financial reporting system which contains a mandated set of disclosure rules? This question was basic to the Advisory Committee's investigation, the most comprehensive analysis of the SEC since its inception. The final report of the Committee answered the question by asserting that required disclosure in financial reports increases the accuracy of information which is released earlier through other sources and, hence, has a "disciplining effect."

To the authors of this monograph, such a contention seemed rather naive, not only because the Report contained no evidence to substantiate it, but also because it appeared to cavalierly dismiss the research on various disclosure rules, particularly segment reporting. Moreover, the Advisory Committee totally ignored the question of evaluating the methods of financial measurement. Even if it presumed that the measurement question is an appropriate activity for the Financial Accounting Standards Board, the SEC is required to exercise oversight of the Board's decisions and indeed, often has done so since the enactment of the Exchange Acts.

One reason the Advisory Committee gave for ignoring the financial measurement question was that an implication of efficient market research is that measurement is not a substantive issue once disclosure occurs. Yet, at the same time, the Committee defended its adherence to the need for mandated disclosure by stating that virtually all of that research had focused only on New York Stock Exchange-listed securities. Regulation has no rudder when efficient market research is invoked to reject the need for mandated measurement and yet, at the same time, its shortcomings are invoked to justify mandated disclosure. Moreover, as made clear in the monograph, whether the market for all securities is efficient is but one of several issues which must be considered in determining an optimal set of financial reporting rules.

These considerations, and the related question of corporate governance which began to appear in the literature of government-business relations, motivated the authors to tie together their recent research on mandated disclosure and measurement with several new strings of thought. In bringing together the two strands of research, the monograph critically explores the tradeoffs which are inherent in the regulation of financial reporting. The analysis suggests that the apparent models used by public and quasi-public policy makers in the field of financial disclosure and measurement are not adequate.

The authors do not point to a model that regulators might use, although it is hoped that the analysis in the monograph will prove useful to further research on this question. What becomes clear is the need to proceed more carefully. The authors agree with former SEC Chairman Roderick Hills that "we must instill in our regulators an appreciation of the therapeutic value of competition and a willingness to temper the . . . urge to regulate relentlessly with economic data that tests the need for regulation."

We are grateful to Sharon Perry and Barbara Ayres for their efficient typing of the manuscript.

Chapter I

Introduction

What effects financial reporting rules have on corporate decisions is a question which has become increasingly important against a background of rising concern with the impact of government regulation on the allocation of resources. Although much of the concern about regulation and the movement toward requiring agencies to issue economic impact statements has been directed at environmental, safety and drug problems, during the 1970s attention began to be focused on the effects of financial reporting rules established by the Securities and Exchange Commission (SEC) and the Financial Accounting Standards Board (FASB). The motivation for this monograph stems from that attention and from the belief that at a time when reporting activity is being subjected to increased scrutiny, it would be useful to extend the authors' research in this area.

The purpose of the monograph is to add insight into the impact of the regulation of financial reporting on corporate decisions, as well as into the broader relationship of government and business as it resolves the question of the nature and the amount of regulation. Toward this end, the monograph examines the process which has led to a policy of increased regulation and presents evidence that challenges those models that appear to have been relied on by policymakers.

Two financial reporting topics are dealt with at length. The first, segment (line of business) reporting, perhaps was the most important change in disclosure requirements by both the SEC and the FASB since the passage of the Securities and Exchange Acts of 1933 and 1934. The second topic, the appropriate method for measuring research and development (R & D) expenditures, although not as controversial as line of business reporting, represents the basic problem of measurement as well as any other issue. Disclosure and measurement are the two fundamental areas of regulation in financial reporting. There now exists a sufficient amount of in-depth research relating to these areas to allow some generalizations about developments in the movement toward increased regulation.

In analyzing the segment reporting and R & D issues, and at the same time relating and generalizing that analysis to other disclosure and measurement problems, it is argued that existing descriptive and normative regulatory models are not adequate, particularly from the point of view of the policymaker. It is the policymaker, whose rules and regulations affect corporate decisions, who is of primary concern.

The monograph is organized as follows: Chapters II–IV and the beginning of Chapter V provide conceptual and background material on the need for regulation, the choice of regulatory systems and past experience since the inception of the SEC. In particular, Chapter II discusses several critical issues concerning the regulation of financial reporting, including the alternative to regulation—a free market system, the relationship between the SEC and the FASB, and the trend toward involuntary uniformity in disclosure and measurement. Competing objectives in the determination of disclosure and measurement rules are addressed in Chapter III. The causes of a potential impact of mandated reporting rules on corporate decisions are the subject of Chapter IV.

The remainder of the monograph examines related empirical evidence. The focus of Chapter V is reporting by segment and the objectives and effects of disclosure requirements in general. In Chapter VI, the controversy and evidence with respect to the economic consequences of measurement rules pertaining to the investment tax credit, self-insurance reserves, foreign currency translation and exploration and development costs in the oil and gas industry are reviewed. This is followed in Chapter VII by a discussion of important issues related to the reporting of research and development outlays, such as small business and innovation, and the arguments for and in opposition to Financial Accounting Statement No. 2 (FAS 2) and its

SEC equivalent, Accounting Series Release (ASR) No. 178, which required that R & D outlays be expensed.

The empirical methodology and results of studies concerned with management attitudes toward the R & D rule, and the effect of the rule on the level and the variability of R & D are reported in Chapters VII and VIII, respectively. Chapter IX examines the relationship between firm characteristics and the choice of R & D measurement methods prior to the imposition of FAS 2 (ASR 178). Finally, the concluding chapter contains a summary of the conceptual framework and the empirical evidence presented in the monograph, emphasizing the implications for rule-making bodies.

Chapter II

The Regulation of Financial Reporting

A central issue in the preparation of financial statements for public corporations is whether financial reporting principles upon which those statements rest need to be determined by a rule-making body because of "market failure" or whether, given time, those principles which the market deems useful will survive. Proponents of increased regulation of financial reporting assert that without the discipline of an authority, either private or public, Gresham's Law will prevail and a "race to the bottom" will ensue. The advocates of a "free market" system assert that the market is the best long run regulator, and, as such, it is the best judge of when and under what conditions diversity or uniformity in financial reporting is required. The problem for the policymaker is to determine whether an observed lack of voluntary disclosure or the presence of several alternative measuring methods is attributable to "market failure" or whether it is attributable to an efficient cost/benefit evaluation by the market.

A. A FREE MARKET SYSTEM VERSUS REGULATION

The justification for not allowing the market to determine the choice of information needed is ascribed to the "free rider" phenomenon whereby it is presumed that the benefits of financial accounting information cannot be confined to those who pay for it because a free market in financial information would be expected to result in less than optimal social demand. This is merely one case in the classic public good analysis where there is an under-production of the public good in the absence of collective action (*Report of the Advisory Committee,* 1977, Chapter XX).

Such a contention, however, overlooks the strong incentives in the competitive capital markets for the demand and supply of information. On the supply side, incentives exist for firms to provide relevant and reliable information, and on the demand side investors can reveal their preferences for the quantity and quality of information by holding shares of those firms satisfying their needs. In equilibrium, each firm will disclose and measure to the extent that such behavior reflects the preferences of its investors. Those investors whose preferences for either the amount of disclosure or the use of particular measurement rules, or both, are unsatisfied can "vote with their feet," assuming that the cost of shifting their portfolios of securities is less than the cost of adjusting the information disclosed (Lev, 1976). However, in the case of mandated disclosure and measurement rules, if the particular set of mandated rules does not satisfy investor preferences, then information adjustment costs may be incurred even when these exceed shifting costs, since the investor's option of satisfying his preferences by changing portfolios no longer exists.

The presence of disclosure requirements suggests that "market failure" exists because there is an insufficient amount of information supplied. With respect to measurement, however, some have contended that if the appropriate amount of information is supplied (disclosed) to users in some form, then, in an efficient capital market, investors can adjust that information using the set of measurement techniques that suits their preferences. Measurement regulation, in this context, is unimportant, "market failure" does not apply, and there is no need to mandate uniform rules (*Report of the Advisory Committee,* 1977, Chapter XX).

Explaining the need for mandating the supply of information, the Advisory Committee (1977) in its study of corporate disclosure used the word "formatting" to refer to measurement rules. Using that term, it wished to convey the notion that a distinction must be drawn between disclosure and the manner in which that disclosure is presented, i.e., the format or measurement rule used. The essential problem, it contended, is whether disclosure is adequate since only that characteristic is related to publicly available information and, in turn, to the equilibrium prices of securities. However, it is noteworthy that this argument was hedged by a caveat in a footnote indicating that perhaps we do not fully understand the importance of formatting. "This [only disclosure affects security returns] assumes that formatting does not convey any information content. This also assumes that formatting does not induce a 'real' effect" (*Report of the Advisory Committee*, 1977, p. 646). Evidence with respect to the "real" effects of formatting is presented in Chapters VI, VIII and IX.

The theory of adverse selection and the asymmetry of information between the buyer and seller, in this case the preparer and user of financial information, may provide insight into the need for measurement rules (Ronen, 1979). In this context, uniformity of measurement is required because management, as any seller of a product, has more information about its firm than the user of the information and therefore it is in a position to select measurement rules which will "fool" the user. As Ronen (1979, p. 423) stated: "We do have arrangements in the American capital market that minimize the adverse selection bias."

Adverse selection does not explain, however, why the capital market needs arrangements to protect the investor. With respect to other products, the reliance on experts acts in part as a substitute for a warranty. Further, where uncertainty exists with regard to the return on an investment, the price of that investment will reflect the uncertainty. In the sale of homes an unknowledgeable buyer must face a knowledgeable seller, and the law does not require "arrangements" to minimize the adverse selection bias. The buyer is likely to discount "cosmetics" in this case, anticipating such activity by the seller. Moreover, he knows that he is protected by anti-fraud laws and that he can hire the services of an expert appraiser. In the case of financial statements, the auditor serves to help make the statements credible and experts such as underwriters, financial analysts and other sources may be relied on for advice.

A less regulated state where a greater number of measurement alternatives exists may permit management to provide better signals concerning the firm's future. It has been argued that the existence of both an efficient capital market and a managerial labor market, influencing lifetime earnings through reputation, serves to "discipline" managers to use measurement methods which provide the most useful information with respect to the firms' expected earnings. Given no restrictions on entry to managerial positions, we should expect that the incremental cost of using an alternative would be equal to its perceived benefits (Ross, 1979).

Even if one is willing to admit that the need for regulation is likely somewhere between the state of total regulation of financial reporting with no management choice and a state characterized by a completely free market for information, a reading of the history of changes of rules since 1933 suggests that those changes seem to have been made on an *ad hoc* basis without explicitly balancing costs and benefits. The movement toward greater regulation in disclosure and measurement, the fundamentals upon which financial statements are formulated, does not seem to have been based on a paradigm of an ideal mix of mandated regulation and market regulation, but appears to have been part of a trend. That trend is toward greater corporate accountability, largely based upon the perception that the market cannot internalize certain social costs.

In fact, since the creation of the SEC by Congress in 1933 we have witnessed, particularly since the early 1960s, a significant increase in the standardization of practices in the preparation of financial statements. That should come as no surprise since the SEC early in its life (1937) announced in ASR 1 that opinions would be published periodically "for the purpose of contributing to the development of uniform standards and practices on major accounting questions." The promulgation of uniform standards is a basic activity for which the SEC was created by Congress.

A key question with respect to this activity, however, is whether a limit exists. Conceivably, all companies in all industries could issue financial statements based on a single chart of accounts which are derived from single measurement and disclosure rules. Such a position has not been stated overtly, but it may be implied by those wishing the federal government to engage in more directive planning, as has been done in France. What has been stated overtly by some is the necessity for the SEC to directly determine uniform standards rather than mediately through the private sector, a process which is perceived to lead to lengthy delays.

What would be useful in this regard, but does not exist, is an economic model of corporate financial information which shows for both disclosure and measurement where and why private benefits are less than social benefits. Such a model should also be able to delineate the conditions for an optimum amount of uniformity, accounting for the fact that mandated standardization of financial information, like any other product, is to some extent likely to reduce its value. In determining net social benefits, such a cost may be relatively small compared to other benefits derived from uniformity. Such an even weak operational model is not extant. In its absence, analyses of *ad hoc* changes in rules have often only vaguely referred to costs and benefits. The measurements, particularly of benefits, appear to have been inadequate and have tended to be subjective.

As is discussed in more detail in section D, both the SEC and the FASB have recognized the need to be more sensitive to the cost/benefit trade-off of rule-making. In 1980, the Board stated:

> Though it is unlikely that significantly improved means of measuring benefits will become available in the foreseeable future, it seems possible that better ways of quantifying the incremental costs of regulations of all kinds may gradually be developed, and the Board will watch any such developments carefully to see whether they can be applied to financial accounting standards. Even if that hope proves to be a vain one, however, the Board cannot cease to be concerned about the cost-effectiveness of its standards (*Statement of Financial Accounting Concepts No. 2*, 1980, par. 144).

The history of standard setting for disclosure and measurement shows that the need to demonstrate benefits, however subjective they may be, arises especially in circumstances where the evidence suggests that unintended adverse effects may result from a mandated rule. In other circumstances, where the economic effects appear neutral, the standard-setting bodies may find it sufficient merely to assert benefits, such as the elimination of noncomparability. Nevertheless, the important issue here is that the use of trade-off considerations by standard-setting authorities is critical and often necessitates that economic analyses be performed.

B. THE RELATIONSHIP BETWEEN THE SEC AND THE FASB

The SEC was created by Congress in the Securities Exchange Act of 1934 as an independent agency to administer that Act and the Securities Act of 1933. A primary function of the Commission is the regulation of disclosure and measurement standards, based largely upon the belief that the securities markets' failure of the 1930s resulted from inadequate disclosure and an excessive number of measurement methods by public companies. These deficiencies, it was believed, led to a sharp decline in confidence by investors and, in turn, significantly contributed to the unprecedented market failure. President Roosevelt, in his message to Congress requesting such legislation, said:

> There is, however, an obligation upon us to insist that every issue of new securities sold in interstate commerce shall be accompanied by full publicity and information, and that no essentially important element attending the issue shall be concealed from the buying public.
> This proposal adds to the ancient rule of caveat emptor the further doctrine 'let the seller also beware'. It puts the burden of telling the whole truth on the seller. It should give impetus to honest dealing in securities and thereby bring back public confidence (Benston, 1976, p. 19).

For this reason the Securities Act of 1933 is often referred to as the "truth in securities" law.

The primary concern of the Acts was the protection of investors, with the intention that such protection would lead to a more efficient allocation of capital resources. Almost 45 years later, a special study group examining the goals and effectiveness of the SEC, restated the same purpose. "The one area that is the Commission's alone is the protection of the investor through disclosure . . . its function is to assure the availability of investor oriented information. To the extent other objectives conflict they must give way" (*Report of the Advisory Committee,* 1977, p. 310).

Since its inception, the approach of the Commission has been to delegate its authority, in part, to the private accounting profession to determine—subject to its oversight—the proper disclosure and measurement rules. In 1938, the Commission by a 3 to 2 vote made this position official in ASR 4.

> In cases where financial statements filed with this Commission pursuant to its rules and regulations under the Securities Act of 1933 or the Securities Exchange Act of 1934 are prepared in accordance with accounting principles for which there is no substantial authoritative support, such financial statements will be presumed to be misleading or inaccurate despite disclosures contained in the certificate of the accountant or in footnotes to the statements, provided the matters involved are material. In cases where there is a difference of opinion between the Commission and the registrant as to the proper principles of accounting to be followed, disclosure will be accepted in lieu of correction of the financial statements themselves only if the points involved are such that there is substantial authoritative support for the practices followed by the registrant and the position of the Commission has not previously been expressed in rules, regulations or other official releases of the Commission, including the published opinions of its Chief Accountant.

This requirement has two elements. First, the SEC will not accept financial statements unless they are prepared in accordance with generally accepted accounting principles (GAAP), i.e., principles having "substantial authoritative support." If such support does not exist then, *ipso facto,* they are false or inaccurate despite any disclosures. Second, if the Commission disagrees with the registrant and the accounting principles used have "substantial authoritative support," the SEC will accept footnotes to the statements (disclosure) in place of changing the statements to the SEC's point of view, providing that the SEC has not previously expressed its opinion on the matter.

These two points are essential to an understanding of the attitude of the SEC toward accounting (disclosure and measurement) principles. First, the SEC restates its right, delegated to it by Congress, to rule against a registrant if it does not follow GAAP as established in the private sector. Second, it reserves the right to determine its own rules.

Historically, the Commission has looked to the accounting

profession for the development and statement of reporting rules. Beginning in 1932, the American Institute of Accountants (AIA), along with the New York Stock Exchange, made the first attempt to recommend accounting principles. It recommended that "the more practical alternative is to leave every corporation free to choose its own methods of accounting ... but require disclosure of the methods employed and consistency in their application from year to year" (AIA, 1934, p. 7). G. O. May, both the accounting advisor to the New York Stock Exchange and the Chairman of the AIA's Special Committee on Cooperation with Stock Exchanges, argued in 1932 that: "The trouble with an 'official' system of accounting is, that while it is possible to lay down broad principles, wide variations are possible within the limits of such principles, and which variation should be adopted is a question on which one cannot rightly be dogmatic" (Zeff, 1972, p. 123).

Following ASR 4 of the SEC, the then American Institute of Certified Public Accountants (AICPA), formerly the AIA, established a Committee on Accounting Procedure (CAP) which began to issue research bulletins in 1939. Forty-two bulletins were issued during the period from 1939 to 1953; eight of these were connected with terminology. The authority of the Committee was tenuous because it itself stated the force of its opinions "rests upon their general acceptability" (Zeff, 1972, pp. 167–173).

Because the progress of the CAP was not considered to be sufficiently rapid, the AICPA established the Accounting Principles Board (APB) in 1959. The function of this new Board was to formulate GAAP and to reduce the number of alternative financial reporting methods. The APB was to rely on persuasion rather than compulsion in achieving these objectives. The basis of persuasion was expected to be a demonstration that a recommended procedure was the best among the alternatives considered.

The APB issued 4 Statements and 31 Opinions during its tenure between 1959 and 1973. It came under criticism because of its alleged slowness, for the quality of the Opinions and the research supporting them and, perhaps more importantly, because the voting members of the Board were all accountants appointed by the AICPA and all working on a part-time basis.

The issues considered by the APB were often controversial, e.g., the question of promulgating criteria for financial measurement in mergers and acquisitions, and some interested groups felt that the impact of the solutions was sufficiently broad to warrant more diverse representation on the Board and more extensive research and hearings. Moreover, the credibility of the APB was weakened at an early stage in its history when the SEC refused to accept an Opinion and forced the Board to reverse itself (see Chapter VI.A).

The result of this was the replacement of the APB by the FASB in 1973, composed of 7 full-time, instead of 18 part-time, members. A new organizational structure also led to a broader representation. The FASB, in the same year it was established, received a vote of confidence from the SEC in ASR 150. This release stated that the principles, standards, and practices promulgated by the FASB in its Statements and Interpretations would be considered by the Commission as having substantial authoritative support, and those contrary to such FASB promulgations would be considered to have no such support.

Thus, since 1973, the FASB has been the rule-making body in the private sector which has had the responsibility for setting standards of disclosure and measurement in financial reporting for all business firms, corporate and noncorporate. The delegation to the FASB by the SEC of the determination of these standards, encompasses public companies only.[1] Yet the effect of standard setting by the Board and its predecessors has been, and is, a single set of rules which apply to all companies, private as well as public.[2] These standards are part of the set of principles used by auditors in the certification process, and therefore are referred to as "Generally Accepted Accounting Principles" (GAAP).

The compulsive force behind the FASB's pronouncements has stemmed from (1) the code of ethics of the accounting profession; and (2) their acceptance by the SEC. Rule 203 of the AICPA's Code of Professional Ethics, adopted in the same year that the FASB was founded, stated:

> A member shall not express an opinion that financial statements are presented in conformity with GAAP if such statements contain any departure from an accounting principle promulgated by the body [FASB] designated by Council to establish such principles which has a

material effect on the statement taken as a whole, unless the member can demonstrate that due to unusual circumstances the financial statements would otherwise have been misleading.

The vote of confidence noted above which the SEC gave the FASB in ASR 150 needs to be placed in perspective. In ASR 150, the SEC stated its expectation that the private standard-setting body would take the leadership "in establishing and improving accounting principles." However, during the FASB's first year, the Board issued one statement while the SEC issued 20 Accounting Series Releases. Although the FASB has had to revoke one important Statement because the theoretical underlying concept was found deficient by the SEC (see Chapter VI.E), no SEC releases have been revoked by subsequent Statements developed by the FASB.[3]

In addition, the SEC's statement of reliance on the private sector must be questioned because in a number of important instances the SEC has initiated action which the FASB later merely confirmed. Thus, in 1970, it was the SEC which mandated line of business reporting, one of the most controversial problems in financial reporting. The Board six years later mandated a similar version in FAS 14. Not yet satisfied, the SEC, one year later, adopted Regulation S-K which in some aspects required more detail than No. 14. A detailed analysis of these events is presented in Chapter V.

Examples of significant financial reporting areas where leadership was assumed by the SEC were:

1. "All Inclusive" vs. "Current Operating" P & L Statement Concept. ASR 70, issued in 1950, established a classification for special items of profit and loss, thus giving support to the "all inclusive" concept. This was confirmed by APB 9 in 1966.
2. Accounting for Leases. ASR 147, issued in 1973, required that the lessee provide supplementary "as if" disclosure of the effect, if material, that would result when non-capitalized leases met certain criteria for qualification as financial leases. In 1976, the FASB, issued Statement 13 which was consistent with ASR 147.
3. Disclosure of the Effects of Inflation. ASR 190 in 1976

required large companies to provide supplemental re-placement cost data. FAS 33, issued in 1979, required as supplementary information both constant dollar and current cost information, the latter being acceptable to the SEC as a substitute for replacement cost.

C. DISCLOSURE AND MEASUREMENT RULES

As noted in section A, a distinction frequently is drawn in financial reporting between rules or statements which primarily concern the release of existing financial data (disclosure) and those activities which affect the determination of the methods by which assets, liabilities, ownership and profit and loss are disclosed (measurement). This distinction, often fuzzy, has been used by the SEC, the FASB and the AICPA. The fuzziness is due not only to the fact that there often is overlap between the two concepts, but also is conditioned by the obvious fact that measurement itself is conducted only because what is measured is considered to be worthy of disclosure.

It has been said that generally the SEC has placed more emphasis on disclosure and has left the problem of measurement to the FASB. Evidence of the FASB's concern with measurement issues is its long term project aimed at the development of a conceptual framework. That task, which has been in progress since 1976, is meant to provide a framework which will help to answer questions such as "what is an asset" and "what is profit" and thereby provide a basis for a consistent set of measurement rules.

In a number of instances in the past, however, measurement problems have not been left in the hands of the private sector but were either answered directly by the SEC, or the resolution of a disclosure question by the SEC also resolved a measurement problem. For example, in 1978 the SEC reached the conclusion that the FASB's solution to the measurement of unsuccessful drilling and exploration costs in the oil and gas industry was not correct and that a type of current value financial reporting (reserve recognition accounting) should be tried for an experimental period of at least three years (ASR 253). As a result, the Board's rule, FAS 19, was revoked (see Chapter V.E). In another instance, the Commission did not accept the

APB's resolution of the single, best method of measuring the tax savings from the investment credit (see Chapter VI.A). These were cases in which the SEC directly determined measurement rules.

Less overt were the cases where the distinction between disclosures and measurement was not explicitly made. For example, consider the "all inclusive statement" rule of the SEC which was referred to in the preceding section. In requiring disclosure of extraordinary and unusual items in the profit and loss statement, this rule also determined how net profit and loss were to be measured. A second example, the issuance of the SEC's ASR 268 in 1979, requiring redeemable preferred stock to be classified as debt rather than equity, was as much a measurement issue as a disclosure one. Also, as earlier noted, FAS 13, requiring lease capitalization under specified conditions, was preceded by the SEC's ASR 147 which required disclosure in the footnotes of what the effect would have been if certain noncapitalized financial leases were capitalized by lessees. In this case, the SEC's disclosure rule led to a FASB measurement rule which brought footnotes into the body of the statements. Thus, the SEC appears to have taken an active role in setting measurement rules as well as disclosure rules.

D. THE TREND TOWARD UNIFORMITY IN MEASUREMENT METHODS

A cardinal objective of the regulation of financial reporting has been to increase the extent of uniformity in financial statements, leading to a reduction of discretion by management in the choice of alternative reporting methods and to an increase in the extent of comparability which is presumably useful to the investor (Keller, 1965).

From the advent of the Committee on Accounting Procedure in 1939 through the existence of the APB and since the creation of the FASB in 1973, each body has expressed a desire to increase uniformity.[4] The FASB, particularly, has spent much time and effort in attempting to derive single, best measurement rules. Thus, the rule-making bodies have not been persuaded that adequate disclosure can resolve measurement questions.

The SEC has been a major force behind the private-sector bodies in the movement toward uniformity because of its belief that confidence by users will be enhanced when unjustified alternatives are eliminated. This belief is grounded historically in ASR 1 of 1937 which stated that opinions on accounting principles would be published periodically "for the purpose of contributing to the development of uniform standards and practices on major accounting questions." Forty-three years later, the SEC's support of the most important project undertaken by the FASB, the Conceptual Framework Project, is based upon the belief that the formulation and promulgation of a set of basic concepts for financial measurement will more readily resolve the difficulties of selecting best methods among alternative practices (SEC, 1980).

A 1977 report by a Congressional Committee ("Metcalf Report") also emphasized the contention that the function of accounting authorities was to hasten the elimination of alternative reporting and measurement practices. A portion of the report expressed dismay and disappointment with the pace of the FASB and its predecessors in achieving uniformity and recommended that the SEC should take a more forceful role to hasten the achievement of uniform practices. As the report stated, "the goal of establishing a system of uniform and meaningful accounting standards, so far, has remained as elusive as ever under the direction of the FASB" (Committee on Government Operations, 1977, Chapter 8).

In seeking uniformity, one may conclude from the Board's position on a number of financial reporting rules that rulemakers tend to focus on the substance of the transaction rather than its consequence or purpose. Hence, as a rationale for treating accounting measurement for the development stage company in the same way as that for an operating company, the Board contended that "the accounting treatment should be governed by the nature of the transaction rather than by the degree of maturity of the enterprise" (FAS 7, par. 30). The fact that for the development stage company the outlay is incurred in anticipation of future revenue, given that it presently has none or hardly any, was not considered critical by the Board.[5]

Uniformity of measurement rules also has been justified by viewing it as a means of reducing management's ability to select rules beneficial to itself but not necessarily in accordance with investor preferences. Uniformity is intended to eliminate "wrong" methods of reporting, to increase comparability of firms and, as a result, to improve capital allocation. In testimony on FAS 19, this argument was made by the Chairman of the FASB, Donald Kirk, when he stated that "... mandating one accounting method ... will foster competition in capital allocation by having all oil and gas producers reporting comparable data ..." (Statement before the Department of Energy to consider Statement No. 19, February 21, 1978). Uniformity is sought as a necessary ingredient for providing improved comparability and creditability ("confidence") in financial statements when like entities are being compared (SEC, 1980, p. 30).[6]

In response to these alleged advantages, critics have argued that when dissimilar entities are being compared, mandated uniformity may lead to incorrect interpretations,[7] and that the elimination of reporting alternatives can affect some firms' investment-production decisions and its ability to raise capital. Evidence in support of the latter contention relates the magnitude of real effects of a uniform measurement rule to firms' operating and financial characteristics (Collins, Dhaliwal and Rozeff, 1979) (see Chapter IV).

Some observers suggest that the underlying reason for uniformity is that auditors prefer to operate in a tightly structured environment which minimizes judgment and thus the risk of legal liability (Lev, 1976, p. 133). An examination of the positions behind the "uniformity vs. flexibility" debate reveals that a major concern has been whether possible legal liabilities would be less under uniformity than under practices which permit alternatives (Bradley, 1965).

More specifically, this issue relates to the general prohibitions against fraud specified in the Securities Acts. Corporate decisions with respect to the measurement of "assets" and "income" are subject to such provisions, particularly where reliance is placed upon management's perception about a future economic event. A prime example of this is the selection of a rule for measuring firm R & D expenditures prior to the time when a single rule was mandated in 1975 (FAS 2). When R & D was capitalized the firm's management, with the certification of the auditor, signalled its belief that future benefits would ensue. If later it could be shown that management's beliefs were unsupportable and that, as a result, users relying on the capitalization method sustained economic losses, charges of gross negligence or intended fraud could be levied against the management and, perhaps, the auditors. Here the issue is essentially whether the measurement rule applied was based upon a reasonable forecast, where "reasonable" is a rather broad term for "business judgment." The reasonableness of the rule in the application to R & D outlays is merely an aspect of the general problem with respect to other capitalization or expensing decisions.

For other measurement rules the issue is less clear. With respect to the choice between full costing and successful efforts accounting in the oil and gas industry, a forecast related to a particular expenditure was not involved since the issue was how to report expenditures for drilling and exploration which were known to have led to dry holes. The same principle applied to the question of the measurement of pre-operating losses by development stage enterprises in FAS 7. The measurement issue in these cases was whether expensing was required because no benefits were forthcoming or whether capitalizing should be permitted because future benefits would not have the same probability of occurring if it were not for the "investments" currently made.

The anti-fraud provisions could not apply in these cases to a forecast of benefits of a particular investment viewed by itself because there were none. It might, however, apply to a forecast for a portfolio of investments or for the company as a whole. That is, when management determines, subject to confirmation by an outside audit and a similar confirmation by its board of directors, that capitalization and subsequent expensing is generally more in accordance with the earnings generating ability of a portfolio of investments or for the firm as a whole, this judgment could be subject to the anti-fraud provisions.

The case most often made for uniformity of measurement standards rests on the alleged need to increase comparability of financial data by detecting similarities and differences of certain characteristics between firms and industries. Toward this end, the selection of a particular measurement method has not been made arbitrarily by fiat, such as an edict that cars should keep to the right side of the road as opposed to the left side. Indeed, the background discussion of measurement rules presented in Chapters VI and VII suggests that rule making bodies mandate a particular method because it is considered to be the best one among available alternatives.

Even when the single "best" method is selected, the Board has recognized that increased comparability is not a goal that can be attained without any costs, and that improving comparability may destroy or weaken relevance or reliability. Nevertheless, no examples or instances of an evaluation of the trade-off between uniformity and reliability have been provided, although the use by some European countries of standardized charts of accounts in the interest of interfirm comparability has been cited as a possible, though arguable, source of reduction in relevance and reliability. How the benefits of improved comparability and the costs of a reduction in relevance and reliability are to be measured or evaluated in a general framework is left unanswered.

Furthermore, recognition has been given to the possibility that "uniformity may even adversely affect comparability of information if it conceals real differences between enterprises" (FAC 2, par. 116). The weakness of such an observation lies in the fact that the meaning of "real differences" (also sometimes referred to as "circumstances") has not been determined. "Real differences" may be inherent in the transaction being reported alone, the consequences of the transaction, or, as discussed in Chapter X, in the characteristics of reporting firms. How "differences" is defined is extremely important.

It is instructive to compare the alleged need for uniformity across firms with the need for uniform financial data by headquarters of a decentralized company. Alfred P. Sloan, Jr., who introduced financial controls in the early growth of General Motors as a decentralized corporation, was concerned about the need for uniformity. He noted that "... The reports, for example, were not usable for evaluation and comparison until they were set up on a uniform and consistent basis. Uniformity is essential to financial control, since without it comparisons are difficult if not impossible" (Sloan, 1964, p. 143). General

Motors of the 1920s was not, of course, as diverse as it became in later years.

A 1965 study of the financial reporting and control practices of decentralized firms revealed results quite contrary to Sloan's idea. Solomons (1965, p. 52) noted that within decentralized firms nonuniformity persists because increased disclosure allows central headquarters to make any adjustments or refinements in order to measure intra-firm performance. As he stated:

> There is one aspect of consistency which might be thought to have special relevance for a divisionalized company, and that is consistency of accounting methods between divisions. Surprisingly or not, very little importance seems to be attached to this kind of consistency by most such companies. It is quite common to find, for example, that some divisions of a company use a LIFO basis of inventory valuation, while other divisions do not. Divisions may use a diversity of depreciation methods. It is less common, but not unknown, to find one or more divisions using direct costing while other divisions use absorption costing.
>
> These inconsistencies reflect, in part, a desire of top management to leave as much room as possible for individuality on the part of divisions. They also imply recognition of the fact that different accounting methods may be appropriate to the diverse needs of the divisions.

Why a single authority, central headquarters of a decentralized firm, allows diversity but rule-making bodies need to impose uniformity of measurement across firms, is not clear.[8] Disclosure is regarded as a substitute for uniformity within the decentralized firm but has not been fully acceptable to the regulators for external reporting.

Consideration of the issues discussed above has been part of the Board's recent attempt to more explicitly consider the costs and benefits of its rules. Special conference studies sponsored by the Board have been concerned with the economic consequences of the establishment of measurement and disclosure rules (FASB, 1978). The recent increase in the substitution of regulation for market-generating forces in the determination of accounting principles or measurement rules has made such studies particularly important. "... [T]he traditional efforts of accounting regulatory bodies [has been to] enhance interfirm uniformity ... [and thereby to reduce] the choice spectrum, and there is undoubtedly an urgent need for research on the optimal balance between regulation and free market forces in the production of financial information" (Lev, 1976, p. 139).

NOTES

1. The reporting requirements apply to public companies with assets over $1 million and over 500 shareholders.

2. Consideration has been given, however, to the need for establishing "little GAAP" and "big GAAP", depending upon company size (*Report of Committee on GAAP,* 1976). Also, the FASB has relaxed the requirements of reporting segment statements and earnings per share for private companies (FAS 21). Chapter III.B contains a discussion of reporting regulations for small business.

3. ASR 163, withdrawn after FAS 34 became effective, did suspend interest capitalization until a decision was made by the FASB.

4. A key item in the objectives of each of those bodies was that a reduction of alternative measurement methods would result from the adoption of policies which would confine variations to those justified by differences in circumstances. To date, however, no clear definition has been assigned to "circumstances."

5. Others have argued that the elimination of managerial discretion under such circumstances impairs the usefulness of the statements because, although in form they are uniform, in substance they lack economic meaning when the consequences of the underlying economic events are excluded (Sunder, 1976).

6. A similar argument centering on "confidence" has been used to justify federal chartering of corporation as a means of eliminating the diverse state laws of incorporation (Nader, R., Green, M. and Seligman, J., 1976, pp. 33–61).

7. For instance, see (United States Department of Justice, p. 18).

8. Although "flexibility" and "diversity" are two terms used to describe the same substance, they have different implications.

Chapter III

Competing Objectives in the Determination of Disclosure and Measurement Rules

This chapter discusses several issues related to the determination of disclosure and measurement rules by policymakers. Section A considers the need for managers to provide financial information ("signals") to investors and how uniformity may affect the usefulness of such information. The attitudes of policymakers to the use of income normalization or smoothing is discussed in section B. Finally, section C describes and evaluates the changes of financial reporting rules for small business.

A. SIGNALLING AND UNIFORMITY

The two basic functions which accounting statements serve are: (1) monitoring of management (historically referred to as "stewardship"), an outcome of the principal-agent relationship; and (2) providing information useful in decision making to investors or potential investors. The first function is based upon contracts such as bonding arrangements, indenture agreements and management compensation plans. Many contracts which require the measurement of financial restrictions or results as a condition of the continuation of the principal-agent relation express their contractual agreements in terms of historically-based or acquisition costs. A bond indenture, for example, may give the right to the lender to demand immediate

23

payment of principal from the firm if the firm's book value of debt to equity exceeds a ratio specified in the contract. The ratio most often is expressed in terms of accounting values according to GAAP.

The second function of financial statements is forward-looking because the information required for actual or potential decisions is information related to the future. One means toward the derivation of such information is an extrapolation of measurement data accumulated in the past. Another, the forecasts of future earnings by management, of course, is a more direct source of this information. Both functions, to the extent that they rely on historic data, could be attested to by auditors. Even in an economic environment which did not mandate the auditing function, it would be likely that it would be undertaken anyway because agency costs would be reduced and the uncertainty surrounding inferences by investors would be minimized.

In instances where management is faced with a choice among alternative reporting methods when a single measurement rule has not been mandated, one factor influencing that choice may be the perceived need of the investor. Signalling management's expectations, either short or long-run, could be a factor in the choice of a measurement method, management knowing that its expectations are useful information for the investor or potential investor's decision model. Of course, credibility of the method used and of the information provided is built up over time or increased through audit attestation. Thus, in selecting methods and providing information, management would have to consider the increased benefit from the use of a method signalling its expectations, the cost of the attestation by the auditor, and the cost of the reduction of wealth for both auditors and the manager if a "false" signal is provided.

Accordingly, when a measurement choice exists, some managements may choose to capitalize certain outlays in the belief that presenting the information in that manner provides the most appropriate signals with respect to future prospects. Those signals, because they are related to management's expectations, clearly are both difficult and costly to audit. In fact, an audit in this case is similar to attesting to, and therefore certifying, a management forecast, a practice which is not currently done.

The imposition of uniformity of measurement, particularly a method that is easily auditable, will serve to reduce direct and indirect (possible litigation) auditing costs, but at the same time the signal most useful to the investor may be removed. Mandated uniformity does not allow management to evaluate the trade-off between the benefits of signalling and the costs of auditing.

The required expensing of R & D, when a choice was available before 1975, serves as a good example. The decision to capitalize R & D when a choice existed may have meant that management's evaluation of the additional auditing costs indicated that they were less than the value of the signal provided. The imposition of a uniform method, expensing, eliminated the ability of management to make a cost/benefit evaluation after 1975.

Although it did not systematically address this particular issue, the FASB recognized that such trade-offs are necessary. For example, in the Board's *Statement of Financial Accounting Concepts No. 2, Qualitative Characteristics of Accounting Information* (1980, par. 134) it is stated that:

> But in the real world the market for information is less complete than most other markets, and a standards-setting authority must concern itself with the perceived cost and benefits of the standards it sets—cost and benefits to both users and preparers of such information, to others, like *auditors* who are also concerned with it, and to anyone else in society who may be affected (emphasis added).

Discussion of actual costs and benefits by the regulatory bodies have referred primarily to users and preparers (corporations). Thus, although it has been recognized that corporations might voluntarily undertake the cost of disclosing or measuring in order to secure benefits from users such as improved access to capital or a lower cost of capital, it was never made clear how auditors affect the cost of preparers or the benefits to users or whether their interest is distinct—forming a triad which requires evaluation.

A hint of this probelm was provided by the vice-chairman of

the Board in a discussion of the genesis of the expense-only rule for R & D (FAS 2). The Board rejected selective capitalization, the most serious contender for adoption as a standard for research and development, because it was "not likely to improve comparability between enterprises, nor to relieve the discomfort of auditors . . ." (Sprouse, 1979).

It is interesting to note that the discomfort of auditors may be a positive function of the size of the company audited. For example, the cost to the auditors of making an error when R & D is capitalized in a large firm may exceed the benefits to the investor of receiving a signal of management's expectation and, in such a case, may lead the auditors to force a conservative position on management. However, the possible costs to the same auditors of a small firm capitalizing R & D may be less, resulting in a greater willingness to permit management to send the signal. Of course, the possibility of making such a choice is eliminated when uniformity is mandated.

B. THE FASB, THE SEC AND INCOME NORMALIZATION

The use of uniformity in financial measurement often has been justified on the grounds that it would eliminate income normalization or smoothing, sometimes less graciously referred to as a form of "manipulation" or "creative accounting." In particular, the uniform methods mandated by the Board and the Commission have been those methods which, because they more closely approximate a cash basis, tend to result in greater income variability.

Numerous statements by representatives of the Board, the Commission, and members of Congress indicate beliefs that management may use, or has used, nonuniformity of measurement methods to smooth income. These statements have been made in relation to many of the reporting questions which the Board has addressed. For example, in FAS 19 the Board stated (par. 156):

> The same issue has arisen in a number of other Board projects, for example, the projects on self-insurance, catastrophe losses, expropriations, and other contingencies [FAS 5] and on foreign currency transla-

tion [FAS 8]. A *basic issue* in each of those projects, as it is in the oil and gas project, was whether financial accounting standards should be adopted to normalize or average the effects of events that are inevitable over extended periods but occur at infrequent and relatively unpredictable intervals. Consistent with its conclusion in this Statement, the Board concluded in those projects that financial statements should report the effects of risk and not attempt to normalize them [emphasis added].[1]

Similar concerns have been voiced in testimony to the Commission[2] and in Congressional studies (Committee on Government Operations, 1977).

Inferentially, the emphasis of the rule-making bodies has been that smoothing is practiced by some companies to lower perceived risk and thus to reduce their firms' costs of capital. Consequently, uniformity is likely to increase the volatility of the earnings streams of these companies, causing their costs of capital to rise. Presumably, the result will be a more efficient allocation of resources because the mandated method has revealed the firm's true risk. In sum, this position assumes that the expected benefit of a uniform method which causes a more volatile earnings stream is that, by providing a better picture of risk, resource allocation will improve.

As was previously mentioned, the behavior model leading to such a conclusion has never been made explicit. To the contrary, economic theory has held that a firms' risk is a function of the uncertainty of its future cash flows. Moreover, with adequate disclosure, those who allocate resources, i.e., investors, could adjust the statements of firms on any basis they deem fit, and thus, in an efficient market, resources would not be misallocated.

The suggestion that mandated uniformity is necessary because it better reveals risk actually implies that measurement standards are rules of conduct meant to restrain unfair economic behavior. Presumably, the manager operating in a world of nonuniformity, will seek unfair advantage over the investor. The investor, in turn, is assumed to be unable to penalize such activities, if performed, by actions he might take in the market. He needs the help of a rule-making authority since the securities markets is viewed as inefficient without uniformity.

The attitudes of all rule-making authorities, however, have

not been entirely consistent with the above view. J. C. Burton, former Chief Accountant of the SEC, a person who has been identified as an activist during the six years he held the position, stated that the regulator himself is a "smoother," identifying this not as "manipulation" but as sensible long-run behavior.

> One of the purposes of regulation is to conform short-run to long-run behavior. Both investors and managers may have their behavior dominated by short-run influences, while the regulator seeks to smooth the impact. This requires judgments as to the long-run interests of investors, and suggests that one of the Commission's functions is to anticipate investors' needs . . . (Burton, 1980, p. 81).

This theme, that management tends to think short-run, is not confined to measurement or disclosure rules. It is the core of the recent debate over corporate accountability (Williams, 1980a). Chairman Williams (1980b) has chastized U.S. business for focusing on short-term performance and he has repeated this theme: "It [U.S. business] rewards short-term performance in too many ways—in terms of incentive compensation, in terms of stock options, in terms of how quarter-to-quarter earnings performance is compared." Perhaps one important reason for his observation, granting its validity, is that the standardization of measurement rules which both the Board and the Commission imposed have contributed to a focus on short-term performance because of its contribution to increases in earnings volatility. Or, stated differently, would the absence of mandated uniform measurement rules, by permitting smoother earnings streams, result in a greater focus by firms and investors on longer term results? That this is an important problem is clear from statements by business analysts that a significant reason for the decline in U.S. productivity is attributable to the increased concern of managers with short-term results.

It is interesting that Chairman Williams in his public statements places the onus of responsibility for the pervasiveness of short-term planning on management, whereas former Chief Accountant Burton allows the inference that if, indeed, management is short-run oriented it may be attributed to the existence of short-term evaluations by investors. There is a clear contradiction between the attitudes of the FASB and that

voiced by Burton. The Board appears to desire that the investor infer long-run behavior from earnings streams which have
become more volatile due to uniformity. Burton, however, believes that the SEC's function is to help the investor by perform-
ing the smoothing function itself, i.e., conforming short-run
changes to the long-run trend.

However, it is more likely that if management smoothed
(normalized) income in the past, as the Board contended, it
did so much more efficiently and capably than the SEC or any
rule-making authority could have done. This would be expected
since management alone is privy to the best knowledge about
the probability of future trends in its income stream. If management did smooth in the past, was smoothing done for the very
purpose which the former Chief Accountant identifies as a basic
activity of the SEC, i.e., to give investors signals of long-range
trends based on current economic events?

The above question is posed to emphasize the lack of clarity
about the purpose of rule-making as it applies to measurement
and disclosure. The result of this is the anomalous situation
whereby the Board, in several Statements, expressed an anti-
smoothing position for management while others appear to
want to extricate the investor from the resulting disadvantage
by undertaking smoothing itself. How such policy is oper-
ationalized is difficult to determine, and it appears that the
situation may be equivalent to the activity of the "Sorcerer's
Apprentice": The harder the FASB works as the agent of the
SEC to eliminate smoothing, the harder others, including the
SEC, will have to work to reinstate it.

Chairman Williams (1980c), criticizing American business for
its emphasis on the "tyranny of the short-run," cites European
and Japanese businessmen as examples of long-term thinking.
Nowhere, however, does he discuss the differences between the
U.S. and other countries regarding the existence of measurement alternatives. It is well known that European countries and
Japan are more permissive with respect to the use of financial
reporting methods. (See, for example, Chapters V.D and
VII.B).

In sum, insufficient attention has been given to the possibility
that uniformity of measurement may itself force management
into emphasizing short-term performance. When the FASB and

promulgate uniform measurement standards which,
of their closeness to a cash basis, lead to a greater
of earnings, they may, in fact, be encouraging man-
t to concentrate on the short-term.

C. FINANCIAL REPORTING REGULATION AND SMALL BUSINESS

During the late 1970s there was an increasing concern by Congress, particularly Senator Gaylord Nelson's Select Committee on Small Business, about the retardation in capital formation by small business (Joint Hearings, 1975). Reflecting this concern, various task forces were established to suggest ways to stimulate capital formation by small business, e.g., the Advisory Committee on Federal Policy on Industrial Innovation. The recommendations of these groups have tended to follow a similar pattern. Most frequently suggested has been a revision of the tax laws, such as raising the surtax exemption or permitting investors to defer capital gains taxes on reinvestment in small business. Also mentioned have been revisions in the laws applying to Small Business Investment Companies, revisions to ERISA with a view toward amending the "prudent man" rule to permit pension funds to make greater investments in small business, and revisions to state and federal regulation in general. Certainly, the need to stimulate small business investment has been widely recognized.

Because of this need and because both evolving practice and empirical research in financial disclosure and measurement distinguish between the effects of rules on business by firm size, the regulation of financial reporting for small businesses deserves special attention. This section discusses particular aspects of the regulation of financial reporting which relate to small business and its ability to raise capital. As indicated, this is one important area in which the regulatory bodies have begun to make exceptions to the imposition of uniform requirements.

As noted in Chapter II.B, to promote its primary function of protecting investors, the SEC and the FASB have developed a mandatory system of disclosure based upon the premise that confidence in the capital markets is enhanced if everyone has equal access to information. With a few exceptions, in the past the equal access doctrine has meant that disclosure requirements were uniform irrespective of firm size.

Nevertheless, recently, and of its own volition, the Commission has demonstrated concern with possible impediments to capital formation which arise from the high cost of compliance with its rules. Formally, a June 5, 1975 amendment to the SEC Act of 1934 has, in effect, required the Commission to undertake an economic study of its own rules:

> The Commission, in making rules and regulations pursuant to any provisions of this chapter, shall consider among other matters the impact any such rule or regulation would have on competition. The Commission shall not adopt any such rule or regulation which would impose a burden on competition not necessary or appropriate in furtherance of this chapter (Securities and Exchange Act, 1975).

In the spirit of this amendment, the SEC's disclosure requirements, particularly as they impact on small business, have come under scrutiny in order to determine whether the benefits alleged for "full disclosure" are offset by the costs to small business of providing additional information. Questions have been raised about the need for uniform disclosure across all firms, particularly when the Advisory Committee on Corporate Disclosure of the SEC revealed that the reporting costs for Forms 10-K, S-1, and 10-Q were almost 200 times more per dollar of sales for small companies (assets less than $100 million) than for large companies (assets over $1 billion) (*Report of the Advisory Committee,* 1977, Chapter XVII).

More specifically, the Advisory Committee found that the average cost per $100,000 of sales for submitting Form S-1 alone, i.e., excluding costs of Forms 10-K, S-7, and 10-Q, was $1,849.91 for a small company with assets less than $100 million compared to $27.30 for a medium size firm with assets between $100 million and $1 billion. No data were given for companies over $1 billion, but a reasonable approximation would be $5.00 per $100,000 of sales.

Not only were disclosure costs significantly higher per sales dollar for the smaller company, but it was learned that there was very little interest by sophisticated (institutional) investors in companies with less than a capitalization of $50-100 million (*Report of the Advisory Committee,* 1977, pp. 514-515). A committee of the AICPA had suggested that disclosure rules had largely developed from a desire by the Board and the SEC to satisfy the demands by financial analysts for information pertaining to large companies. That committee, concerned with the reporting problems of small business, had stated:

> Although some types of financial information may at times be considered necessary to meet the needs of certain user groups, this fact by itself should no longer be considered to create a presumption that the reporting of such information has become an integral part of GAAP to be applied to *all* business enterprises (emphasis added) (*Report of Committee on GAAP*, 1976).

It appeared, then, that a reduction in disclosure requirements for small companies would result in a cost savings by reducing compliance costs without necessarily affecting benefits.

Many respondents at the SEC public hearings on problems of small business had complained about costly registration and reporting rules. As a result of this and the evidence collected by the Advisory Committee on Corporate Disclosure, the SEC amended several rules which were judged to be unfairly burdensome on small firms. A major step was taken when the Commission allowed small companies offering securities in amounts between $1.5 and $5 million to use a simplified form of registration, Form S–18, which significantly reduced their legal and accounting costs. Previously, all companies were required to file on Form S–1, the Commission's most elaborate and most costly registration form.

There have been several other amendments in disclosure rules based on size. In 1975, the SEC amended its 10–Q requirement for interim reports (ASR 177) stating that "the greatest investor need for these data exists in the case of such companies whose activities are most closely followed by analysts" (i.e., only larger companies). In 1976, the SEC exempted companies with less than $100 million of inventory and gross plant and equipment from reporting on a supplemental replacement cost basis in ASR 190. Also, FAS 33 on price level accounting exempted companies with less than $1 billion of assets. Finally, as mentioned earlier, the FASB no longer requires nonpublic companies to disclose segment earnings or earnings per share (FAS 21).

Another sign that consideration is being given to the impact

of disclosure requirements on small business is the recent establishment of the Office of Small Business Policy within the SEC:

> The great concern which the government has today for the well-being
> of small business stems from the vital role it plays in the general econ-
> omy. The contribution of small businesses in supplying jobs, technical
> innovation, and generally in keeping our system competitive requires
> that unnecessary obstacles to their formation and growth be re-
> moved ... The [new] Office of Small Business Policy [of the SEC] will
> have primary responsibility for developing and assisting in the de-
> velopment of rules and regulations designed to assist and ease capital
> formation (Karmel, 1979).

Chairman Williams of the SEC has emphasized that securities
regulations, which in the past have been evaluated strictly on
the basis of investor protection, now must also be judged on the
basis of the impact they may have on the ability of small businesses to raise capital: "The task of identifying the impact of
Commission regulations on small businesses and of assessing
the extent to which any rule revisions designed to assist small
business may impair the protection of investors on such ven-
tures entails a careful balancing of these two related, but separate, national goals" (Williams, 1978). With this in mind, the
Commission also is considering creating a small business class
whose reporting burden under the continuous reporting section of the 1934 Act would be significantly reduced.

Clearly, the Commission and the Board have recognized that
disclosure need not be uniform with respect to firm size. Surprisingly, little, if any, attention, however, has been given to
whether measurement rules, themselves, as distinct from the
level of disclosure, should be uniform. As is the case for uniform disclosure rules, uniform measurement rules also may
impact unfavorably on smaller companies. The specific reasons
for this and the types of effects which uniform measurement
rules may have on small firms are discussed in Chapter IV.
Evidence of changes in firm behavior accompanying FAS 2, the
R & D measurement rule, is provided in Chapters VIII and IX.

NOTES

1. In August 1980 the Board issued an Exposure Draft proposing a revision of FAS 8 which, among other recommendations, would require that
foreign currency translation gains and losses bypass the profit and loss state-

ment until realization occurs. Such a recommendation would, if required, enhance income smoothing relative to the alternative mentioned in the quotation.

2. Harold Williams (1980d), Chairman of the SEC, in an address at Northwestern University stated that a major concern of companies required to use current value accounting (Reserve Recognition Accounting) in the oil and gas industry or required to use replacement cost accounting (ASR 190) if above a certain size (approximately $1 billion of assets) was the tendency for the new method to "lead to greater volatility and lesser predictability of reported earnings."

Chapter IV

Potential Causes of Impact of Measurement Rules on Firm Behavior

This chapter explores several reasons for possible firm reaction to mandated measurement rules. Factors considered include agency theory, management compensation schemes, exchange listing requirements, government contract evaluation procedures and inefficient markets and income effects. Each of these is discussed in terms of its effect on a firm's investment, financing and dividend decisons when measurement rules change.

A. AGENCY THEORY AND MANDATED RULES

The work by Jensen and Meckling (1976) which proposes a theory of the firm founded on agency relationships, and the later work by Fama (1980), provide useful insights into the contractual relationship of managers and outside providers of capital. Implicit and explicit contracts exist between the principals or providers of outside capital and the managers, or agents. The existence of these contracts requires a monitoring process that depends upon, among other factors, the measurement of key accounting variables and their verification by independent auditors. Among the important conclusions of Jensen and Meckling is that the financial structure of the firm is not independent of the existence of these contracts.

Two types of contract changes which may affect the equilibrium position of firms are relevant to changes in measurement rules. Bond indenture agreements have restrictive covenants, the majority of which are written in terms of generally accepted accounting principles. Many firms also have compensation contracts with key managers which include bonus plans that also are defined in accounting terms. Changes in accounting techniques, such as the required switch to the expense-only rule for reporting R & D (FAS 2), by mandating a different system for measuring key variables, can effectively change the provisions of these contracts and thereby affect the firm's equilibrium position.[1]

The mandated switch to the R & D expense method in 1975 reduced the equity of affected firms both currently and retroactively since R & D could no longer be treated as an asset. With the decrease in equity there was a corresponding increase in the ratio of debt to equity. Because lending agreements often include provisions which specify maximum debt/equity values, Statement 2, may have led to technical defaults requiring loans to be renegotiated. Even if not violated, such covenants would tend to be more restrictive. As a consequence, the mandated switch may have affected the ability of firms to raise debt or to lease in the future (Fogelson, 1978; Leftwich, 1980).

In addition, to protect the bondholder, indenture agreements have restrictions on the minimum relationship of accounting earnings to interest expense on long term debt. A violation of this minimum caused by the mandated switch to expensing could have occurred because of a relatively large decline in accounting earnings.[2]

Bondholders also protect their wealth by including in agreements restrictions on dividend payments to equity claimants. Since these restrictions are usually expressed as a percentage of accounting earnings, affected firms might be required to make smaller dividend payments in the future than had been planned for, as well as to reduce current dividend payments or renegotiate the loans. It is important to emphasize that renegotiation would not be costless. The costs of renegotiation include incremental transaction costs, and in some cases, the cost of borrowing at a higher rate of interest caused by changes in interest rate levels or firm risk since the time that the original loan was arranged.

Besides affecting protective covenants, lower earnings and

asset levels caused by the rules may affect budgets and financial statements that provide a means of evaluating the firm's performance by new suppliers of external capital. In addition, the information contained in financial statements often is used as a means of determining the size of a manager's compensation. In particular, information such as the level and variability of the firm's earnings stream often is the basis for determining the size of management bonuses, the value of profit-sharing plans and promotion decisions within the firm. Therefore, it may be hypothesized that the manager may alter the firm's financial and/or operating decisions in response to changes in reporting rules which decrease the level or increase the volatility of the firm's earnings stream in order to "protect" his remuneration.[3,4]

Not only may the manager's current compensation be tied to earnings, but accounting results are likely to be used by the managerial labor market as a means of evaluating his reputation and therefore adjusting his future wages. Thus, for this reason also, the manager has an immediate interest in the size and direction of a change in earnings and the way that the change will be used and interpreted.

Borrowing and managerial compensation contracts could be written in ways that would leave them unaffected by accounting changes, depending only upon generally accepted accounting principles existing at the date of the contract. However, this approach would be costly to the firm because of the need to keep a different set of reports for each contract written that would be different from the report distributed to the firm's equity holders and the SEC. In practice, it appears that because of the substantial cost of maintaining different reporting systems, the provisions of most contracts are written in terms of generally accepted accounting principles which change over the lives of the contracts. Therefore, the effect of those provisions would be altered by changes in measurement principle such as those specified in Statements 2 or 19.

Because the firm's investment and financing decisions have an immediate effect on the aforementioned monitoring measures, i.e., key financial accounting levels and ratios, any change in these measures caused by measurement rules may affect the firm's operating and financial decisions. For instance, with respect to the debt covenants discussed above, even if they are not violated, they may tend to be affected in such a way that the firm's capacity to issue additional debt would be more limited. For this reason, the firm's financing decisions may be affected.

Equally important, any reduction in earnings brought about by a measurement rule may constrain the dividend decision as noted above and affect the firm's choice of investments. Thus, management may adjust its investment portfolio in order that its expected earnings stream will be less likely to cause a violation of any covenant. For example, the expense-only rule for R & D may have prompted management, knowing that the full effect of an R & D outlay will be reflected in its firm's current statements, to reduce planned R & D and change the pattern of future expenditures in order to "cushion" the rule's adverse impact on the firm's financial constraints.

B. SUPPLIERS, LISTING REQUIREMENTS, AND GOVERNMENT CONTRACT AWARDS

The establishment of constraints on a firm's activities as a means of monitoring the firm in order to prevent wealth losses is a concept that is not confined to the customary relationships which firms have with bondholders and residual claimants. Suppliers, securities exchanges and government agencies also establish similar implicit constraints to protect their loans, reputations and awards or grants. For these reasons unfavorable changes in the monitoring constraints may adversely affect a firm's ability to continue to receive or to increase trade credit from its suppliers, to continue to maintain or to seek exchange listing for its securities, or to obtain government contracts. Even if these externalities would not occur, management may have perceived they would occur and acted accordingly.

To consider these factors further, let us continue to focus on Statement 2. With respect to listing requirements it is important to observe that the majority of companies affected by this rule had securities which were traded over-the-counter. To facilitate accessability to the capital markets, these companies would either desire to seek membership in the National Association of Securities Dealers Automated Quotation system (NASDAQ), or, if already a member, to remain in the system, or perhaps to qualify for listing on the American Stock Exchange (AMEX).[5]

Both the NASDAQ and the AMEX systems have initial listing and maintenance requirements that would be negatively affected by Rule 2 and thus could prevent listing or cause delisting.[6] There is no automatic waiver because of changes in the measurement of a firm's financial position caused by FASB (SEC) rule changes, and although a hearing can be requested when a firm is delisted, the cost of the hearing, if permitted, is borne by the firm.

Similar to potential problems related to listing requirements, negative changes in accounting numbers and ratios might impair a firm's ability to receive government contracts. One of the attitudes expressed by the financial officers surveyed in a study discussed in Chapter VIII was that Rule 2 would create difficulty in the evaluation of their firms' performance by government agencies. The results showed that even 53 percent of officers from firms which had been expensing (those that would not be affected by the rule) believed that "some or considerable difficulty" would be created for government agencies in evaluating the performance of affected firms. More importantly, among deferral firms (those affected), the percentage was even higher (71 percent).

Both the FASB and the SEC have stated that, in setting measurement and disclosure rules for financial reports, their concern is to provide useful information to the investor and creditor. Research in the past on financial reporting rules has been devoted entirely to the impact on investors by means of analyzing securities returns or the impact on creditors by an examination of changes in bond values.

Unlike investors and creditors, government agencies are not wealth maximizers. Also, decision makers in agencies are more likely to be risk averse than those in the private sector because the personal awards for successful decisions are not as large nor as immediate. As a result, it would be expected that there is a greater inclination for such decision makers to exhibit "functional fixation," i.e., to focus on accounting numbers rather than cash flows.[7]

Financial capability is an important element in the pre-award survey (PAS) conducted by government agencies on all firms which bid on contracts.[8] Presently the financial evaluation performed is judgmental, though each agency has guidelines appearing in their policy and training manuals. Each sets out general suggestions about the acquisition and use of financial information. It appears that there is a special wariness about small, rapidly growing companies because of the perception that the risk of overextending financial resources is greater, and that these companies frequently have limited capital and often are poorer risks than large companies since they are less able to absorb financial losses.

As a consequence, the use of financial ratios tends to become an important element in assuring contracting agencies against default by contract proposers. Although such ratios are also used by lenders, they are likely not as important because the lender, unlike the contracting agency, can attach various constraints to assure performance on the loan, e.g., restrictive covenants, higher interest rates and liens. The Defense Logistics Agency Manual, for example, indicates that, while all PAS functions are important in evaluating proposed contracts, the pre-award financial capability review is critical for determining capability to perform.

The use of financial ratios is central to the determination of capability by governmental agencies. Thus, the financial analyst is expected to evaluate, among a large number of indicators, such ratios as: total liabilities/net worth, net profit/tangible net worth (10 percent is considered desirable according to the Defense Logistics Agency manual), net profit/net sales, net profit/working capital and other ratios where either the net profit or the net worth (perhaps corrected for intangible assets) appears.

As noted above, financial analysts using these ratios have a tendency to be risk averse, since they likely bear the risks of positive recommendations of companies unable to successfully perform on contract awards but not the risks of negative recommendations of those firms which might have successfully performed. Hence, there may be a greater inclination by the financial analyst and contract officer to reject contract proposals when key ratios became suddenly more unfavorable. However, as was earlier suggested, even if in part this were not so, the managements of small firms may have perceived it to be so, and thus may have been less inclined to submit as many contract proposals, or to reduce the size of those submitted when ratios were negatively impacted.[9]

The authors have made a preliminary investigation of the effect of Rule 2 on contract awards briefly discussing the issue with financial analysts at NASA, SBA, DOD and HEW. Impressions vary, and this may be partially attributable to different agencies. All the individuals contacted indicated that poor financial ratios are one important factor leading to negative recommendations, while a few said that they (not necessarily others) would explicitly adjust the statements of those companies being reviewed that were affected by FAS 2. The financial ratios affected by Rule 2 were extensive; all ratios with net profit in the numerator were often sharply reduced, and the leverage ratio, debt to equity, was often sharply increased. Thus it appears that measurement rules may affect the contract evaluation decisions of government agencies. This question warrants further research.

C. EFFICIENT MARKETS AND INCOME EFFECTS

Efficient market theory suggests that the securities markets do not react naively to "cosmetic" changes in accounting numbers but only to real events. Accordingly, measurement changes such as those mandated in Statement 2, would not be expected to significantly alter security price distributions except in instances in which they are accompanied by changes in disclosure or in cash flows.[10]

Accepting the efficient market hypothesis, the Advisory Committee on Corporate Disclosure (Sommer Committee) has emphasized the importance of mandated disclosure rather than measurement rules (*Report of the Advisory Committee*, 1977, Chapter XX). Similarly, others have stressed repeatedly that the FASB should not devote resources to seeking the "best" measurement rule; rather it should concentrate on extending and improving disclosure. For example, with respect to the investment tax credit, Beaver (1973, p. 53) argued that "Potential harm is not likely to occur because firms use flow-through or deferral for accounting for the investment credit. Rather, the harm is more likely to occur because firms are following policies of less than full disclosure. . ."

Most of the evidence in the finance and accounting literature supports the efficient market hypothesis. Nevertheless, two other possibilities related to market efficiency are suggested as explanations for possible effects of uniform measurement rules on management's decisions. First, management may believe that a lower and less stable earnings level caused by a rule would result in lower security prices and a higher cost of capital, a belief which is borne out by the questionnaire results reported in Chapter VIII. Whether, in fact, lower security prices and higher costs of raising funds would occur is a separate issue since measurement rules may have had an impact on the perceptions and decisions of the preparers of the financial reports (managers) without necessarily directly affecting the users of the information (security market participants). In fact, the market may actually have ignored a change such as the R & D switch because it provided no change in expectations about cash flows, yet management may have believed otherwise.

That a measurement rule such as Statement 2 can significantly lower the reported income of affected firms is shown by the results of two tests reported in Table IV.1. Using a sample of firms which is described in detail in Chapter IX, the z scores, significant at the .001 level, indicate that if those firms that had

Table IV.1. Results of Wilcoxon Matched-Pairs Signed-Ranks Tests to Determine Whether Use of the Expense Method for Reporting R & D Would Have Reduced Reported Income Prior to the Mandated Switch in 1975

		DEFERRAL GROUP		
Test Variable	*n*	*+ ranks (mean)*	*− ranks (mean)*	*z score*
$\overline{Y_A - Y_R}$	43	9 (16.33)	34 (23.50)	3.936****
$\overline{(Y_A-Y_R)/Y_R}$	43	10 (19.40)	33 (22.79)	3.369****

Variable Definitions: $\overline{Y_A - Y_R}$ = mean of adjusted income minus reported income
$\overline{(Y_A-Y_R)/Y_R}$ = mean of adjusted income minus reported income to reported income

Note: One Tail Tests
*   significant at the .10 level
**   significant at the .05 level
***   significant at the .01 level
**** significant at the .001 level

been deferring R & D prior to 1975 had instead used the expense method, earnings would have been significantly lower. For these firms use of the expense method would have resulted in an average earnings decline of 97.2 percent and a median decline of 15.1 percent in the period 1970–75.

Tests also were conducted to determine whether the expense-only rule would affect income variability. As in the test on income levels, a determination was made as to whether the rule would have changed the variability of income if, instead of deferring R & D outlays, firms expensed prior to 1975. Two variables for the R & D companies were used to test for differences in the variability between the adjusted and reported incomes of affected firms; the variables were the absolute value of the actual change in the percentage change of net income and the absolute value of the percentage change in the percentage change of net income (Table IV.2). The insignificant test results for both measures suggest that the null hypothesis that there would have been no difference in income variability if deferral companies instead had expensed R & D cannot be rejected.[11]

Another possible reason Rule 2 might have affected management R & D decisions relates to the efficiency of the markets for small companies' securities. It is important to note that relatively few studies have dealt with small firms not listed on the major exchanges, such as the large majority of those affected by Statement 2 or those which would have been affected by Statement 19. Furthermore, as the methodological procedures used in market studies improve, researchers have begun to find a number of inconsistencies that cruder data and techniques missed in the past.[12] Although unlikely, based on previous evidence, it is possible that security market participants may react negatively to lower and more volatile earnings figures and to higher financial leverage ratios of small firms caused by uniform measurement rules. In an effort to mitigate this type of reaction, the managements of affected firms may have attempted to offset the changes in reported numbers of reducing R & D expenditures or changing their pattern.

Making the above possibility regarding Statement 2 extremely important is the fact that successful, small high-technology firms such as those affected by No. 2 often grow at a

Table IV.2. Results of Wilcoxon Matched-Pairs Signed-Ranks Tests to Determine Whether Use of the Expense Method for Reporting R & D Would Have Reduced the Variability of Reported Income Prior to the Mandated Switch in 1975

Test Variable	n	+ ranks (mean)	− ranks (mean)	z score
		DEFERRAL GROUP		
$\overline{\text{actual } \Delta}$ in % Δ Y A-R	43	25 (21.52)	18 (22.67)	.785
$\overline{\dfrac{\%\Delta}{\text{in } \% \Delta \text{ Y}}}$ A-R	43	23 (22.96)	20 (20.90)	.664

Variable Definitions:

| actual Δ in %Δ Y| A-R = mean of the absolute value of the actual change in the % change of the difference between adjusted and reported income

| % Δ in % Δ Y | A-R = mean of the absolute value of the % change in the % change of the difference between adjusted and reported income

Note: One Tail Tests

   *   significant at the .10 level
   **   significant at the .05 level
   ***   significant at the .01 level
   **** significant at the .001 level

high rate, perhaps as much as four times greater in sales than mature companies and are highly dependent on external sources of funds to finance growth. Even when compared with small, nontechnological firms at the early stages in their life cycle, these firms rely more heavily upon external sources for growth. For instance, at the time of their first public offering, less than one percent of the funds generated by small high-technology companies come from internal sources as compared to about 25 percent internally generated by small non-technological firms (see Figure IV.1). In addition, small technological firms receive about 48 percent of their funds from the equity market as compared to 14 percent for the other group (*An Analysis of Venture Capital Market Imperfections,* 1976, p. 18).

Although small R & D firms are highly dependent on external capital, surveys of financial analysts have revealed that there is very little institutional interest in companies with less than $50–$100 million capitalization (Financial Analysts Federation, 1977). Thus it is likely that a high proportion of equity holders of small companies are "unsophisticated." Figure IV.2 supports this contention, revealing that for the small high-technology firms the portion of equity raised from "unaffiliated" plus "unknown" sources is about 40 percent.

Because of the importance of funds supplied by "unsophisticated" investors, a financial accounting change such as Rule 2 may be more likely to either have led the market to revalue affected firms because of a decline in reported earnings, or to be perceived to do so by managers. Responding managers, in turn, may have reduced their R & D investment outlays in

Figure IV.1. Composition of Sources of All Financing for a Sample of Small Firms Making Initial Public Offerings 1970-1974

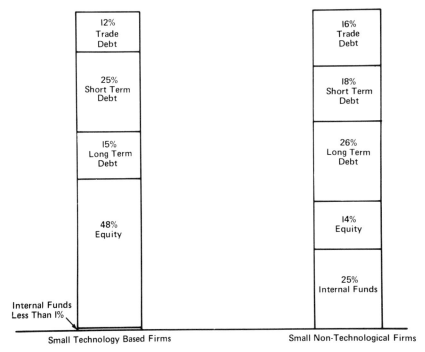

Small Technology Based Firms   Small Non-Technological Firms

Source: An Analysis of Venture Capital Market Imperfections, National Bureau of Standards, Boston, Mass.: Charles River Associates, 1976, p. 18.

Figure IV.2. Average Composition of External Funds Received by Small Technology Based Firms (percentage distribution by type of investors)

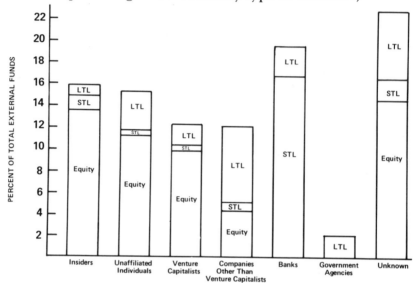

Notes: LTL = Long term loans
STL = Short term loans

Source: An Analysis of Venture Capital Market Imperfections, National Bureau of Standards, Boston, Mass.: Charles River Associates, 1976. p. 11.

order to offset partially the lower earnings that resulted because of the rule.

The questionnaire results reported in Chapter VIII relate to this point. About 93 percent of chief financial officers of deferral firms expressed the belief that Statement 2 would cause at least some difficulty for unsophisticated investors in their evaluation of deferral firms. Even 75 percent of expensing firms surveyed felt this way.

Similar beliefs were expressed shortly after the Board's rule on R & D when it issued Statement 7 on the accounting and reporting for developing stage companies (FAS 7, 1976). The issue here was similar to the R & D issue, i.e., whether to require deferral or expensing for the financial reporting of pre-operating costs. And here also, although support for an expense-only rule was expressed by a number of institutional investors and venture capital firms, a high percentage of these investors believed that a mandated switch "might have an impact on the investment and credit decisions of unsophisticated investors" (FAS 7, 1976, par. 49). Thus, the possibility exists that the capital markets for the equities of small firms are either inefficient or are perceived to be so by managers.

Finally, during the hearings before the SEC on the appropriate method of measuring the costs of exploration and drilling activities, several representatives of the largest investment banking firms testified that the capital markets for many growth-stage firms were inefficient. That is, they believed that for the small, growing oil and gas company it could become more expensive and more difficult to raise capital because of the lower reported earnings that would result from mandated expensing ("successful efforts"). As discussed in Chapter VI, that mandate, which was expressed in FAS 19, was later overruled by the SEC.

To summarize, because of perceived or real market inefficiencies, managerial compensation schemes, restrictions in borrowing arrangements written in terms of generally accepted accounting principles, stock exchange requirements or government contract evaluation procedures, changes in measurement rules may affect management's investment and financing decisions. In this manner, measurement rules may have indirect, but nevertheless, important effects on a firm's economic decisions.

NOTES

1. Collins, Dhaliwal and Rozeff (1979) have found that variables related to contract changes partially explain the negative returns observed on the securities of oil and gas firms which were to be required to switch to successful efforts accounting under FAS 19.

2. In section C the magnitude of the decline in earnings is reported for a sample of firms affected by FAS 2.

3. In their survey of FAS 8 ("Accounting for the Translation of Foreign Currency Transactions and Foreign Currency Financial Statements") Peat, Marwick, Mitchell and Co. reported that 26 out of 28 companies asserted that their employees' bonuses and salaries will be increased or decreased because of the accounting changes stemming from Statement 8.

4. The effect of accounting rules on R & D expenditures because of the structure of management compensation plans has been suggested by the Battelle Memorial Institute. See *Probable Levels of R & D Expenditure in 1978,*

Forecast and Analysis, Columbus, Ohio: Battelle Memorial Institute, December 1978, p. 6.

5. Of a sample of 43 affected OTC firms discussed in Chapter IX, it was determined that 15 were listed on the NASDAQ system.

6. Examples of minimum requirements for initial inclusion of an issue of domestic stock on the NASDAQ system are total assets of at least $1 million and capital and surplus of at least $500,000. One of the requirements of the AMEX is pre-tax earnings of $750,000.

7. That government agencies may exhibit "functional fixation," was suggested by Ijiri, Jaedicke & Knight [1966].

8. More than one third of R & D in the private sector is sponsored by the Federal government.

9. A 1980 study of the costs to small business of government rules and regulations stressed the importance of perception by owner/managers. "In many cases, the small business *perception* of requirements may have more impact than the actual cost of these requirements" (Cole and Teleger, 1980, p. 71).

10. Changes in cash flows may occur when measurement methods are mandated for tax reporting as well as for financial reporting. However, this was not the case with respect to many measurement rules, such as Statement 2. Since 1954 the tax code allowed companies to expense R & D for tax purposes even though deferral was used for financial reporting purposes.

11. It should be noted that because of the rather short time period for which R & D data were available, actual percentage changes were used to measure variation rather than standard deviation.

12. In reviewing a number of recent efficient market studies, Jensen (1978, p. 95) stated: "We seem to be entering a stage where widely scattered and as yet incohesive evidence is arising which seems to be inconsistent with the (efficient market) theory.... [W]e are beginning to find inconsistencies that our cruder data and techniques missed in that past ... [T]hese pieces of evidence begin to stack up in a manner which make a much stronger case for the necessity to carefully review both our acceptance of the efficient market theory and our methodological procedures."

Chapter V

Controversy and Evidence With Respect to the Economic Consequences of Disclosure Rules: Segment Reporting Regulation

This chapter discusses the issue of mandated disclosure with emphasis on the disclosure of profit by segment. It contains a review of the historical development of current practices of segment disclosure and evaluates the current state of knowledge about its usefulness. The discussion is restricted to uses of segment data by investors and creditors, and thus excludes uses by agencies concerned primarily with the determination of industry structure, e.g., the Federal Trade Commission.

The chapter is divided into five major sections. Section A considers the need for disclosure rules as opposed to the alternative, a voluntary system. Section B is devoted to the central issues behind current practices in segment reporting. Section C consists of a review and an evaluation of empirical research during the past decade on the value of segment information to investors, and section D suggests a hypothesis to explain segment reporting requirements as they exist today. The final section of this chapter presents a summary and offers suggestions for future research.

Of particular importance are the following questions which are addressed: (1) What were the reasons for mandating segment reports for publicly-held corporations? (2) What have been the major changes in segment reporting since 1970 and why were they made? (3) Does the research on segment reporting requirements provide evidence that these reporting requirements were justified? (4) Does the mandate on segment reporting and its amendments provide insight into the balance to be struck between private and governmental regulation of financial disclosure?

Segment reporting or line of business reporting has been among the most interesting and controversial subjects in financial reporting for several decades. Virtually all groups expressing an interest in financial reports (preparers, users, and auditors) have taken strong positions on either its usefulness or its harm. Segment reporting, unlike some other issues in external reporting, e.g., restructuring of debt or oil and gas accounting, is not limited to a single industry or a few industries and, more importantly, the issues involved are basic and encompass many of the problems that have been raised for other external reporting questions. As the Advisory Committee on Corporate Disclosure to the Securities and Exchange Commission (1977, p. 380) has said, "Few issues . . . have been as enduring or as controversial as that of segment reporting."

As noted in Chapter II, there are two basic problems in financial reporting: measurement and disclosure. The two are conceptually separate, yet from a practical viewpoint they are interrelated because of the need to measure what is disclosed or to disclose what is measured. Thus, though disclosure of profit by segment is conceptually the same as disclosure of aggregate profit for the firm, the difficulty of measuring "true" profit and profitability rapidly increases as the segment definition is more refined and, as a result, the allocation of common costs and transfer price problems become more complicated.

Even if measurement was not a problem, there would still be the need to determine the extent of disclosure that would be required to satisfy both the needs of the users as well as the preparers. This is a difficult problem because these groups see different advantages and disadvantages associated with the amount and detail of disclosure. Thus, it is important to consider the following additional questions: How do we know whether the incremental effort of preparers associated with measuring and disclosing segment information to various user groups, particularly investors, is justified? Are we able to separate the justification from the practical question of precision of measurement? Given the constraints of the auditing rules, are segment reports reliable and/or relevant?

Before proceeding to review recent developments in segment requirements, in order to address these questions, let us briefly consider the alternative to regulation, a voluntary system. It may be noted that just because segment disclosure by all public multi-product firms was not forthcoming under a voluntary system, it cannot be concluded that the existing system was not working.

A. THE ALTERNATIVE: A VOLUNTARY SYSTEM

In a voluntary system of financial reporting it is to be expected that some companies will not disclose. However, if market participants deem segment reporting important for a particular firm, they will interpret the lack of disclosure by that firm as "bad news" and will reduce their willingness to buy that firm's shares; therefore, lack of disclosure should lead to a higher cost of equity capital for the nondisclosing firm relative to a similar disclosing firm. Presumably, under this system the costs and benefits as well as the level of disclosure would be determined in the market place jointly by corporations and investors.

With respect to segment profit reporting as well as many other areas of financial disclosure, however, there seems to be little inclination to allow market forces to work. One reason which has been given is that the voluntary solution is thought to be too distant. The Advisory Committee (1972, p. XXI) has said, ". . . even if it were true that over the long run the market would penalize issuers which withheld useful information . . . frequently the 'run' is indeed long." Aside from the fact that there is no empirical evidence to support this assertion, it has a fundamental flaw. It is difficult to understand why the required release of financial information of firms voluntarily withholding it is presumed to have an immediate effect, but the failure to voluntarily release such information is thought to have only a long run effect. In other words, it is believed that the lack of voluntary disclosure is assumed by the market to be equivalent to "no news" rather than "bad news" in the short run, even though at the same time some other firms are voluntarily disclosing. The "no news" of the short run is assumed in the long run to be transferred into "bad news," although the mechanism by which this occurs is not made clear. Perhaps, in fact, any lack of immediate investor reaction to the nondisclosure of certain information reflects the zero or negative market price of that information.

Another reason for not relying on voluntarism is ethical rather than economic and, hence, is difficult to evaluate. "Confidence" in the securities market has been asserted to rest upon the public's notion of "fairness," and "fairness" is related to the "equal access" doctrine. Under this doctrine it is assumed not "fair" when only some firms voluntarily disclose segment profit, and for those firms not disclosing, presumably only "insiders" or large investors with sizeable resources have access to such information. Thus, a former chairman of the Commission made the following statement about segment profit reporting: ". . . the fact remains that when some companies were reporting this information and some were not, there was an element of unfairness and possible competitive advantage" (Sommer, 1974).

"Equal access" with respect to disclosure is similar to "uniformity" with respect to accounting measurement. If its imposition results in a change in allocative efficiency, judgments can be made about its value. If, on the other hand, it results in wealth transfers because processing costs are transferred between affected groups, then judgments are ethical. Both "fairness" and "confidence" are difficult to deal with unless they can be directly or indirectly measured. That mandated "sameness" is "fair" or increases "confidence" is, then, merely a matter of opinion. Further, "equal access" stemming from mandated disclosure assumes that all parties, insiders and outsiders, will have the same quality of information, i.e., that timely disclosure can be mandated.

Related to the "equal access" argument for increased disclosure is the ascendant attitude about corporate democracy, the auditor as a fiduciary of the public and the special responsibilities of the corporation as a "creature of the state." At a conference on corporate disclosure (*Corporate Financial Reporting*, 1972), Professor W. Mueller, formerly chief economist of the Federal Trade Commission (FTC), clearly stated the point:

"... the formulation of appropriate financial reporting standards for corporations is only one part of the larger issue of the rights and obligations of the large corporation. Indeed, nothing less is at stake than the continued social legitimacy of the modern corporation ... Most Americans seem to have forgotten that business corporations are created by and survive only as a special privilege of the state ... corporate secrecy—not corporate disclosure—is the great enemy of a market economy. ..."

A similar point was made by another former chief economist of the FTC (Scherer, 1979), also in connection with the need to have mandated segment profit reports. He stated that: "... there is a difference between individual living persons and corporations, and that grant of a corporate persona (sic) by the state imposes obligations transcending those of warmbodied citizens."[1] As shown in the brief historical review of segment reporting which follows, these and other related views led to a rejection of voluntary disclosure for increased mandated requirements.

B. HISTORY AND REVIEW OF PRACTICES

The review which follows is primarily concerned with segment reporting as it developed beginning in the mid-sixties. What arose during that period was a perceived need for segment data on profit and profitability rather than segment revenue or sales. The latter had actually been required by the SEC since the mid-thirties in filings by registrants. Form A-2 (later S-1), the general purpose form for registering securities, as early as 1937 contained a provision for disclosing the major classes of gross sales. Also, beginning in 1949, Form 10-K required that the registrant indicate the relative importance of each line that contributed at least 15 percent to the enterprise's gross sales (Twombly, 1977). As a result of this requirement, there are early instances of companies incorporating segment revenue data into their annual reports.

The need for segment reporting (profit and profitability) was recognized in 1965 during an investigation of conglomerates by the Subcommittee on Anti-Trust and Monopoly of the Senate Committee on the Judiciary (Rappaport and Lerner, Appendix A, 1969; Plum and Collins, 1976). The SEC, under pressure from the Senate, then began to consider whether the need should be converted into a requirement. The possibility of SEC involvement in establishing rules prompted the Accounting Principles Board (APB) of the American Institute of Certified Public Accountants (AICPA) to issue Statement (not an Opinion) No. 2 in September 1967, "Disclosure of Supplemental Financial Information by Diversified Companies." The Board expressed an unwillingness to require compliance based upon established guidelines for segmentation at that time, preferring to wait until research showed (1) a need by investors for such data; (2) whether the data were reliable for investment decisions; and (3) whether such data were necessary for a fair presentation of the statements.

Taking note of the demands by financial analysts, however, the Board, along with the Financial Executives Institute (FEI), did urge diversified companies to voluntarily consider issuing such information and noted that already there was an increasing trend for information on segment revenue and segment profit and profitability to appear in annual reports.

Although at that time there was scarcely any research on the subject, data gathered by the AICPA supported the contention that there was an increased trend toward voluntary disclosure. Of 600 firms surveyed for fiscal 1968 in *Accounting Trends and Techniques,* there were 69 cases of segment profit breakdown in annual reports. At the profit level for years following 1968 there were the following number of companies for each year: 107 in 1969, 162 in 1970, 196 in 1971, 247 in 1972, 271 in 1973 and 340 in 1974 (Twombly, 1978).[2]

Notwithstanding the emphasis initially placed by the APB and the FEI on voluntary segment disclosure, the SEC, following the recommendations of the Wheat Report (1969), began requiring comprehensive reports on lines of business in registration statements filed on or after August 14, 1969. (The Wheat Report had advocated a requirement, asserting that segment revenue and "to the extent feasible, profits, [were of] crucial importance to security analysis"). In October 1974, the SEC extended the disclosure requirements to cover corporate annual reports to stockholders. It is likely that the expectation of these requirements played some role in stimulating voluntary disclosure in annual reports prior to 1974.

The SEC's initiative raised doubts about the seriousness of the Commission when it stated in ASR 150 in December 1973 that "the Commission intends to continue its policy of looking to the private sector for leadership in establishing and improving accounting principles and standards through the Financial Accounting Standards Board (FASB) with the expectation that the body's conclusions will promote the interests of investors." It had been contended that for segment profit reporting the problem was that voluntarism could not work, that compulsion was necessary and that the APB was incapable of imposing the necessary requirements. Thus, action had to be taken by the SEC (Sprouse, 1979).

This attitude presumes, of course, that there was no doubt that segment profit reporting was necessary and that the APB was "foot dragging." What is implied is that the private sector's call for further research on the usefulness of segment profit reporting and the additional urging for voluntary reports ("jawboning") were merely screens by the APB based on self-interest. This scenario offers another example of when government regulation was thought to be necessary because allegedly voluntary self-regulation was not forthcoming. However, as discussed in section C, the SEC and the FASB may have been too precipitate.

The action taken by the SEC prompted the FASB to place the issue on its agenda. The Board also was persuaded to act because of a 1972 survey of professional financial analysts indicating that segment data were used extensively in evaluating diversified companies and that these data resulted in improved earnings projections in some cases (Financial Analysts Federation, 1972). In addition, other stimuli were the concern by the FTC with the need to evaluate competitive performance, and that agency's proposal for a line of business reporting program in 1970 (McNamar, 1974).

In May 1974, the Board issued a Discussion Memorandum, received position papers, and held hearings that resulted in a September 30, 1975 Exposure Draft (ED), "Financial Reporting for Segments of a Business Enterprise." After additional comments and hearings, a final statement, FAS 14, was issued in December 1976, and became effective for financial statements for fiscal years beginning after December 15, 1976.

FAS 14 justified segment disclosure on the basis that it would improve the prediction, i.e., reduce forecast errors, of company results, presumably profit and profitability. This was assumed necessary because:

> The broadening of an enterprise's activities into different industries or geographic areas complicates the analysis of conditions, trends, and ratios and, therefore, the *ability to predict* [emphasis added]. The various industry segments or geographic areas of an enterprise may have different rates of profitability, degrees and types of risk, and opportunities for growth. There may be differences in the rates of return on the investment commitment in the various industry segments or geographic areas and in their future capital needs (par. 59).

Two reasonable inferences from such an assertion are: (1) forecast errors for predictions of one-product companies were less than errors for multi-product companies prior to the mandated requirement; and (2) forecast errors of multiproduct companies not voluntarily disclosing were less after the requirement than before. These important issues will be considered in section C. First, however, let us compare the critical features of (1) the 1970 SEC Line of Business (LOB) requirement for the 10–K; (2) the 1975 FASB ED; (3) Statement 14 (1976), and Regulation S–K of the SEC (1978).

1. Segmentation

The areas of significant differences among the four segment pronouncements are outlined in Appendix V.1. The remainder of the discussion in this section focuses on the issues listed in the Appendix.

The most critical issue is the determination of a basis for defining and reporting the activities of a diversified firm. Suggestions have been made that the basis of segmentation should be product lines or markets, industries, areas of managerial responsibility and geographical areas (Mautz, 1968, Chapter 3). The present system of segmentation seems to be a compromise between management that sees disadvantages in detailed reporting and the financial analysts who claim that there is a significant value to a detailed breakdown of a diversified firm's activities.

The Advisory Committee on Corporate Disclosure to the SEC recognized that the issue of the basis of segmentation is the most difficult issue because of the severity of measurement problems. That Committee was impressed by the dissatisfaction of financial analysts after about three years of experience with line of business reporting in SEC Form 10-K. Approximately half of the financial analysts surveyed by the Financial Analysts Federation stated that they needed more detail than what was being reported.

The Committee reviewed the arguments set forth by the analysts and management and concluded that the quality of segment information could be improved. Accordingly, the Committee not only recommended the endorsement of FAS 14 because it more precisely defined a segment and made the reported information subject to auditor review (the segment data required by the SEC was unaudited), but it also requested continuation of the 1970 requirement for product class information within the industry segment.[3] (The latter was not required by FAS 14.) Recognizing the increased difficulty of common cost allocation and transfer pricing, however, it recommended that only revenue information be required for product class. The above recommendations were subsequently incorporated in SEC Regulation S-K.

2. Observed Practice in Segmentation

What has been the effect of FAS 14 and SEC Regulation S-K on the "fineness" with which segments are defined? The initial impact of No. 14 was on the 1977 annual reports, and the initial impact of Regulation S-K (and ASR 244) was on the 10-K's and annual reports for 1978.

Two studies (Ernst & Ernst, 1978; Arthur Andersen, 1978) have tabulated the extent of segmentation. Considering only manufacturing and the extractive industries, in both studies the average number of segments per firm in 1977 was found to be 3.5. For those same industries, the average increase in segments over 1976 was 26 percent, with metal manufacturing showing the largest increase of 80 percent. A review of 1978 annual reports (Arthur Andersen Briefs, 1979), however, shows that for the same sample of companies, only seven percent of them further increased the number of segments, and that these companies increased the number of segments by an average of 1.5. This increase was confined to those five industries singled out by the Commission in ASR 244. Thus, the overall increase in 1978 over 1977 was minimal.

With respect to geographical segments, the application of the materiality standard leads to a significantly fewer number than using an industry basis, despite the fact that there may be a greater dispersion of risk, profitability and growth among geographical areas. Furthermore, in determining the required degree of segmentation of foreign operations into geographical areas, a comparison is made with worldwide totals including domestic operations, not with only foreign operations. Thus, a company with slightly less than 20 percent of its operations in foreign operations would report no more than one geographical segment outside the U.S. Fifty percent of a sample of large companies that reported geographical segments in 1977 showed two or three segments. A typical division was U.S., Europe, and Other, or U.S., Canada, and Other (Arthur Andersen, 1978).

Thus, we may conclude that the extent of segmentation by industry and geographical area is, indeed, very modest. As a result, many of the other issues such as common cost allocation and transfer pricing are less difficult to deal with than under conditions of greater segmentation, such as that required by the FTC.[4] It may be noted that the FTC had stated that for its line of business program, the *average* manufacturing firm among the 500 largest would have 11 lines of business with a likely maximum of 53 for some very large firms (McNamar, 1974).

3. Intersegment Revenue

Intersegment and intergeographic revenue data and the basis used for pricing are required to be disclosed by FAS 14. SEC Regulation S–K goes beyond this and requires disclosure of the effect of transfer pricing on the segments' or areas' revenues and operating profits and losses when the basis used for transfer pricing is "*substantially* higher or lower than those charged to or received from unaffiliated parties ... [and] is *material* to an understanding of the segment information" [emphasis added].

How extensive was intersegment revenue reporting for 1977? According to one survey (Arthur Andersen, 1978), over one-half of 250 companies surveyed reported either no or an immaterial amount of such transfers. Of about 100 companies that reported intersegment transfers, 75 percent reported that the basis used was fair market value, and the remaining 25 percent described their policy as "cost," "cost plus a percentage markup," "market less a discount," and "negotiated rates." In another survey of annual reports (Ernst & Ernst, 1978), confined more to manufacturing industry than the previous survey, 63 percent disclosed intersegment sales, and of these, about one-half reported that these sales were at market price.

Several observations which pertain to the conditional S–K requirement on disclosure of the effect of transfer pricing on revenue and profit are of interest. First, no guideline is provided for identifying the meaning of "substantially higher or lower prices." Almost any definition of market price could be made to fit a meaning of "not substantially different." For example, intersegment sales could be made at market prices net of advertising, commissions, credit costs, volume discounts, etc., and this net price is likely within the meaning of "market price."

Such a conclusion seems reasonable when one looks at a similar instruction in the previous 1970 SEC Line of Business rule which called for disclosing the method and effect of pricing intracompany transfers if they "materially affect the reported contribution of a line of business." In fact, few such disclosures were made under this rule. Even if difficulties with quantifying "substantial" are overcome, "material" must also be defined or guidelines provided (see Section B.1). The above observations may be academic because, as previously noted, very few such disclosures are likely.

4. Common Cost Allocation

It would be reasonable to argue that segment profitability is dependent upon common cost allocation (Mautz, 1968, p. 29) and that the investor should be provided with information about the allocation method(s) used so that, if he wishes, he can reconstruct the segment's profit and loss statements using a better method or one which is consistent with other firms. Yet SEC S–K and FAS 14 require only that a "reasonable" method be used, and this method need not be disclosed. Under the SEC's previous 1970 line of business rule, the method and effect of allocating common costs was to be disclosed if "it materially affects the reported contribution to income of a line of business." However, few, if any, such disclosures were made, yet no explanation is apparent as to why it was not extended to the S–K.

5. Major Customer

The concern for investors by both bodies also led to another disclosure difference, the reasons for which are not clear. The FASB requires disclosure of the fact that a segment derives 10 percent or more of its revenue from a single customer or group of customers. The SEC requirement, however, extends this disclosure by requiring that the customer or group be named.

6. Foreign Operations

Although No. 14 and S–K require that depreciation expenses and capital expenditures be disclosed by industry segment, neither require such disclosure by geographical area. Since knowledge of capital expenditures by geographical area would seem useful, its exclusion is puzzling. Only about six percent of 180 randomly selected manufacturing companies voluntarily revealed their capital expenditures by geographic area in their 1977 annual reports (Arthur Andersen, 1978).

7. Interim Reporting

Quarterly reporting for segments has been a controversial issue. No. 14 originally required quarterly data when complete financial statements were issued, but this requirement was later revoked until a special study on interim reporting in general was completed. The SEC accepted this revision. The Advisory Committee on Corporate Disclosure, however, strongly supported 10-Q quarterly disclosure requirements for segments, because analysts place a premium on timely data, and with quarterly segment reports they would be able "to update their earnings forecasts and to assess on a reasonably current basis the impact of economic and political events on sectors subject to different economic and political risks" (Advisory Committee, 1977, p. 390).

Apparently because of strong opposition by industry, particularly because of the short 45 day filing requirement for the 10-Q (the 10-K requires 120 days), the SEC did not incorporate it as a requirement in Regulation S-K.

8. Research and Development

Another controversial issue was the question about disclosure of R & D outlays by industry segment. Single-product companies must disclose R & D outlays in registration filings and 10-K's pursuant to ASR 125 of 1972; therefore, it could be considered "unfair" for diversified companies not to report the R & D outlays of their segments.

The ED did require disclosure of these outlays if they were significant and if they were important to an understanding of the reportable segment. Perhaps, because of the concern by companies that disclosure of such data might impose competitive disadvantages, even under such flexible constraints, both No. 14 and Regulation S-K excluded it.[5]

9. Auditing

As mentioned above, a crucial problem for all the foregoing issues, and one that is frequently overlooked, is the expected precision of the segment data under the constraints of the auditing requirements. (The data for 1970 line of business reports of the SEC did not have to be audited.) As previously noted under several issues, a key term is "material." The materiality standard is established by the auditors (AICPA), not by the FASB. The Statement on Auditing Standards (SAS) 21, *Segment Reporting*, says: "The auditor examining financial statements in accordance with generally accepted auditing standards considers segment information . . . in relation to the financial statements *taken as a whole,* and is not required to apply auditing procedures that would be necessary to express a separate opinion on the segment information" [emphasis added] (SAS 21, 1977). It further states that: "The auditor's standard report would not refer to segment information unless his examination revealed a misstatement or omission . . . relating to segment information that is material in relation to the financial statements *taken as a whole . . . .*" [emphasis added] (SAS 21, 1977).

A "qualitative" criterion is mentioned in the auditing standard that allows a judgment on materiality "as a whole," even though unspecified quantitative thresholds are not reached. Also, such qualitative words as "important," "distort," and "pervasiveness" make the standard quite subjective and, therefore, questions about the precision of segment data, and hence its usefulness, have been raised (Goldwasser, 1978).

To attest to the fairness of segment results based on a measure of materiality "at the segment level" would lead to significantly higher auditing costs. A decision to use "statements as a whole" as a measure of materiality implies that the incremental usefulness to investors of segment attestation is not worth the additional auditing costs.

Some concern has been expressed that the combined effects of (1) FAS 14, that requires that the transfer price used internally be the price that is used to report externally; and (2) SEC S-K, that requires the disclosure of market prices under rather loosely specified conditions, as previously described, may pressure companies into using market prices internally (Schiff, 1979). Based upon our previous discussion of standards of "substantial" and "material," it appears that few firms will disclose market prices separately in conformity with S-K.

Evidence exists (Schiff, 1979, pp. 228–229) that there has been a shift from using cost-based transfer prices to market-based transfer prices in internal operations. Several explanations for such behavior are possible. First, internal and external segmentation are not required to be consistent, and for most firms there is a significantly larger number of internal organizational units than segments (Mautz, 1968, p. 49). These units may still be using cost-based transfers. When they are aggregated into segments, however, a relatively greater use is probably made of market-based transfers without changing the practices of the individual units. Secondly, the terms "market" or "approximate market" are not clearly defined. Some companies report that their intersegment sales are "accounted for at prices comparable to unaffiliated customer sales." Under such a condition, a cost-based transfer price could be used internally although the disclosure by No. 14 of the transfer price basis could describe it as a price that is "comparable to the market." Thus, the consistency requirement of No. 14 seems quite flexible.

Having examined the nature of differences among existing segment reporting requirements as well as having traced their historical development, let us turn our attention to the effects of those requirements on investor decisions.

C. EMPIRICAL RESEARCH ON THE RELEVANCE OF SEGMENT INFORMATION TO INVESTOR DECISIONS

Recently, the FASB has shown increased concern about assessing the costs and benefits of its standards. This is manifest in its Discussion Memorandum on Reported Earnings which has been issued as part of the FASB's review of the form and content of earnings reports, and in its Exposure Draft on Qualitative Characteristics. The latter devotes an entire section to costs and benefits, emphasizing that the standard-setting authority must "... identify and weigh, however subjectively, the probable costs and benefits to preparers and users. . . ." It also identified auditors as a third group whose costs and benefits would be considered. Both of the above documents are part of the Board's work on the development of a conceptual framework.

The Discussion Memorandum associates disclosure requirements generally with the "... *likelihood* that users will be able to make improved assessments of future earnings and cash flows and hence make better investment decisions..." [emphasis added] (p. 27). With respect to segment reporting, in particular, the Memorandum states: "Disclosure of information by segments is ... *likely* to enable users to make improved assessments of future earnings" [emphasis added] (p. 62). This latter statement is a repetition of the following assertion that was made earlier in FAS 14 and which, as shown below, is subject to question. "The purpose of the information *required to be reported by this Statement* is to assist financial statement users . . . by permitting better assessment of the enterprise's past performance and future prospects" [emphasis added] (par.5). Let us now consider the evidence.

Although the empirical studies on segment reporting have differed substantially by sample, by methodological approach, and by type of segment information examined, the general objectives and important issues which each addresses are similar. The most fundamental issue is the effect of the availability of segment information on the allocation of resources in the economy. Resource allocation depends on the cost of capital to firms which, in turn, depends on the perceived risks and expected returns by investors and creditors. If disclosure by segment alters investors' assessments of these variables as reflected in the securities markets, such disclosure may lead to a more efficient allocation of resources.

Research in this area has sought to identify the role that segment data have in the securities markets, both at the aggregate market level in the determination of security market-clearing prices and at the decision making level of the individual market participant. Although often not made explicit, the underlying objective of this research is to determine whether the availability of segment information affects resource allocation via changes in security prices induced by changes in investor decisions.

Table V.1 classifies the relevant research studies according to methodological approach. Existing studies have been classified into two general groups: Indirect and Direct. As noted earlier, many proponents of segment disclosure claimed that disaggregated data on a multi-activity firm permit capital market participants to predict more accurately a firm's future earnings and cash flows than could otherwise be done using only consolidated information. The indirect tests examine this claim by evaluating the ability of investors to make more accurate predictions using segment data. As indicated in Table V.1, these indirect studies can be divided into those which report results on: (1) the accuracy of forecast models; (2) the accuracy of analysts' forecasts; and (3) the efficiency of the securities market with respect to segment information. These studies are

Table V.1. Empirical Research on the Relevance of Segment Information to Investor Decisions

Indirect Studies Based on the Ability to Predict Income		Direct Studies Based on Security Price Adjustments		
Accuracy of Forecast Models: Segment-based vs. Consolidated-based	Accuracy of Analysts' Forecasts: Prior vs. Post Disclosure	Efficiency of Market With Respect to Segment Information (Prior to Disclosure)	Impounding of Future Earnings Information in Security Prices	Impact of Release of Information on Security Risk and Return
Kinney (1971) Collins (1976, 1976a)	Barefield and Comiskey (1975) Barefield, Comiskey and Snyir (1979)	Collins (1975)	Kochanek (1975) Griffin and Nichols (1976)	Collins and Simonds (1978, 1979) Dhaliwal (1978) Horwitz and Kolodny (1977, 1978)

characterized as "indirect" because they do not assess the impact of segment information on the securities markets directly but assume that if earnings forecasts are altered, security prices will be affected. Central to the six indirect studies to be examined is the following question: Does the ability of the investor to make earnings forecasts improve when segment data are available?

The remaining studies in which security market effects are evaluated have been divided into (1) those which examine how quickly and accurately future earnings information is impounded in security prices, and (2) those which measure the impact of the release of segment information on security risk and return.

The next section begins our review of the empirical work. As each study is considered, it is important to keep in mind the kind of segment information each of the authors gives attention to (sales, income, asset, etc.), where that information has been disclosed (annual reports, Form 10–K, etc.), and whether it has been made available voluntarily or involuntarily.

1. Accuracy of Earnings Forecast Models: Segment-based vs. Consolidated-Based

One approach to forecasting the earnings of an n-segment firm is to aggregate the earnings forecasts for each segment where these forecasts have been made on the basis of n time series models, one for each segment. An alternative approach is to predict earnings on the basis of one time series model which uses only consolidated data.

The purpose of the research discussed in this section is to determine whether market participants are able to make better earnings forecasts employing the segment approach. This research assumes that if segment-based prediction models yield better forecasts than consolidated-based models, disclosure of this information is useful to investors.[6]

It can be shown that the earnings of a multi-segment firm (similar to a portfolio) can be predicted more accurately than those of a one segment firm (a single security) because of the diversification effect. In addition, that there are circumstances under which more accurate predictions may be made by utilizing aggregated data than by utilizing segmented data has been demonstrated by Barnea and Lakonishok (1980) and Grunfeld and Griliches (1960).

With respect to the specific data required by the FASB and the SEC, questions have been raised regarding the usefulness of the segment approach to forecasting because of potential data contamination. This contamination is perceived to arise because of difficulty in classifying firm activities into segments and the arbitrariness of transfer pricing and joint cost allocation. Because of these problems, it is possible that the use of segment data may lead to invalid forecasts as well as inappropriate interfirm comparisons.

In addressing the immediate issue, i.e., the determination of the level of aggregation which provides better forecasts, researchers have made the following comparisons. The *earnings* forecasting accuracy of models which use disaggregated *sales* data has been compared to the accuracy of models which use consolidated sales figures. Secondly, the earnings forecasting accuracy of models which use disaggregated earnings data has been compared to the accuracy of models which use consolidated earnings figures. Finally, on the basis of the above analyses, comparisons have been made between the forecasting accuracy of models that use both disaggregated earnings and sales data and the accuracy of models which use disaggregated sales data alone.

Kinney (1971) examined twenty-four companies which voluntarily reported subentity sales and earnings data in 1967, four years before the SEC's 10–K requirement. Using four expectations models to make predictions of 1968 and 1969 company earnings, he found that models based on segmented *sales* data and a firm-wide profit margin permitted better mean forecasts of earnings than the use of aggregated data. However, with respect to company earnings data, he found that once sales figures are known, little improvement is provided by the knowledge of earnings by segment. That is, the predictions produced by segment earnings models were no more accurate than models based on segment sales data and firm-wide margins.

Collins (1976, 1976a) extended the work of Kinney by examining the forecasting issue for a much larger sample of firms, ninety-four. Also, whereas Kinney's sample of firms voluntarily disclosed segment information in annual reports before the SEC mandate, Collins' multisegment sample did not report segment information prior to being required to do so in 1971 in Form 10-K.

Collins (1976a) compared the accuracy of seven consolidated-based models (the two proposed by Kinney plus five additional ones) to two segment models for 1968, 1969 and 1970. The procedure used by Collins to obtain segment-based forecasts was quite different from that used by Kinney. A crucial input was industry sales projections published by the Department of Commerce in *U.S. Industrial Output*. Predictions were made by (1) assigning weights to the different industry segments of a firm on the basis of product line breakdowns in Form 10-K; (2) estimating total firm sales by multiplying the weights as determined in (1) by the sales growth projections for corresponding segments made by the Department of Commerce; and either (3a) applying the overall profit margin of the firm to the aggregate sales estimate or (3b) applying individual segment profit margins to the sales figures estimated in (2) and then aggregating. For each of the three years studied, forecasting accuracy was determined by computing the absolute forecast error as a percent of actual reported earnings. These errors were then averaged over the three test periods.

The results obtained were consistent with Kinney's. In general, more accurate predictions were elicited from the models which utilize disaggregated sales information. However, no significant improvement was exhibited when disaggregated earnings data were used.

> Moreover, the main advantage of segment data appears to accrue from segment revenue disclosure, since predictive ability was enhanced only nominally when segment profit margin data were utilized in addition to segment revenue data. This suggests that arbitrary allocations of joint costs may limit the reliability and predictive usefulness of segment profitability data.... Investors should avoid placing undue reliance on segment profit figures as presently reported under SEC guidelines (Collins, 1976a, p. 126).

Further evidence on the accuracy of segment-based versus consolidated-based forecasts is reported in Collins (1976). In that research the same seven consolidated models and two segment models were employed. However, in this case first-differences of both sales and earnings were entered into the models, and tests were conducted to judge the accuracy of both sales and earnings forecasts rather than just earnings as in Collins (1976a). It was found that "segment based forecasts of sales levels are significantly more accurate than are the consolidated based forecasts. . . ." (p. 174). Yet, once again, with respect to earnings forecasts, segment earnings data provided virtually no marginal benefit over predictions based on segment sales data.

In sum, the cited studies generally suggest the superiority of forecasts produced by segment sales models when compared to consolidated models, but the inclusion of segment earnings numbers contributed little to additional accuracy.

Before proceeding to related empirical work, it is important to note the potential limitations associated with the foregoing line of research. First, we might inquire as to the validity of the hypothesized models. Are they or similar models actually used by investors (analysts)? If, in fact, there exists another set of models which investors rely on and which perform better than the models hypothesized, the conclusion that the disaggregated models tested outperformed the aggregated models tested may have little or no relevance to actual investor behavior. Undeniably, the presumption of the authors that historical earnings are at the basis of future earnings expectations is sound. Nevertheless, the precise process by which past earnings are factored into future projections together with other variables is not clear, but is certainly very critical.

Consider, for example, the dependence of forecasts on non-firm variables in the methodology of Collins. What, in fact, was being tested in that study was whether the joint set of segment firm data, combined with government projections of industry sales, provided more accurate forecasts than consolidated firm data alone. By including government sales projections as input to the segment model only, implicitly it was assumed that the forecaster using the consolidated model had no insight whatsoever about the product lines within a firm (presumably not even the predominant product line) and more generally, that no other source of information was important. Thus, he was assumed to rely strictly on time series models which employed only consolidated historical earnings data.

The questionable nature of this assumption is a reflection of a more fundamental problem which pertains to this avenue of research: the lack of generalizable results. Although it is possible to conclude that segment data are more useful than non-segment data for a specific set of models, it cannot be concluded that this relationship holds for other models nor that it holds with respect to actual investor experience. As Foster (1978, p. 10) points out, what would be of greater use are analytical models which indicate the "conditions under which disaggregation may improve or impair forecasting ability. With such models, one could then examine the properties of the data available and ex-ante predict the consequences of aggregation on predictive ability."

2. Accuracy of Analysts' Forecasts: Prior vs. Post Disclosure

The studies reviewed in the preceding section suggest that disclosure of segment data (at least segment sales data) potentially can be utilized to improve earnings forecasts. Because of the limitations noted, however, the question of whether predictions have improved as a consequence of required disclosure cannot be resolved using the approach of those studies.

A more direct approach is offered by Barefield and Comiskey (1975). Rather than evaluating the performance of hypothetical segment and consolidated earnings models, Barefield and Comiskey directly analyzed the effect of segmented profit data on the accuracy of earnings forecasts made by security analysts. More specifically, they sought to ascertain if the enactment of the 1970 SEC requirement mandating disclosure of segment earnings data (1) had an effect on the average prediction error (bias) made by analysts and/or (2) whether the requirement changed the level of consensus among analysts. Average error (bias) was defined as the square of the difference between the mean of the analysts' forecasts and actual earnings. Consensus was defined as the square of the difference between each individual forecast and the mean forecast. In addition, these measures were used to determine whether forecasting accuracy was greater or less for multi-product firms as compared to single product firms before the requirement.

Predictions made by security analysts and compiled in the Standard and Poor Earnings Forecaster Service were tracked between 1967 and 1972 for a sample of multi-segment firms listed on the New York Stock Exchange. Analogous data were collected for a control single-segment sample of New York Stock Exchange firms.

Barefield and Comiskey found no evidence to support the claim that the average forecast error was reduced when segment profit data became available in 1971. "[D]ata were examined to see if forecasting performance [of analysts] improved as a result of the implementation of the disclosure requirement. Again, no significant impact was noted on bias [average error] scores" (p. 19). Their results did indicate that there seemed to be increased agreement (consensus) among analysts with regard to a firm's future earnings subsequent to 1971. Similarly, there was no evidence that analysts were less able to forecast earnings for multi-segment companies than for single-product firms prior to 1971, although the consensus among analysts was greater for the single segment sample.

In an extended study, Barefield, Comiskey and Snyir (1979) found no improvement in either the level of forecast error or consensus: ". . . the test results at this point do not suggest that the LOBUR mandated by the SEC . . . impacted favorably on forecasts of earnings. This is true whether one examines either the level of forecast error or forecast consensus" (p. 30).

One caveat should be noted concerning the time series approach used in these studies. It must be recognized that factors other than the availability of segment data, e.g., changes in the prevalence of management forecasts or increased disclosure requirements in general, can affect the accuracy of analysts' forecasts. An implicit assumption in the time series tests is that such factors either remained constant over the period examined or affected the control group in an identical manner.

3. Trading Rule Strategies Conditional on Segment-based Forecasts

Another study of the relationship between segment disclosure and investor behavior, also based on forecasting accuracy, is presented by Collins (1975). The underpinning of this work is the association between earnings changes and stock returns reported by Ball and Brown (1968). Ball and Brown compared security returns of firms with positive earnings changes to security returns of firms with negative earnings changes. Returns were observed for a period of twelve months prior to formal earnings announcements to six months subsequent to those announcements. As hypothesized, it was found that for cases in which actual earnings were greater than expectations, security prices increased, whereas in cases where actual earnings fell short of expectations, security prices declined. Of particular importance was the finding that most of the price adjustments to annual earnings (85 to 90 percent) occurred in the twelve month period prior to their announcements. To summarize, Ball and Brown's study revealed that earnings data are important to security valuation, but that for the most part, this information is both available to market participants and impounded in security prices prior to its formal release in annual reports. This behavior was later confirmed by other studies, e.g., Beaver and Dukes (1972).

The findings of Ball and Brown imply that an investor could realize abnormally large security returns if (1) he could anticipate the sign of the unexpected change in earnings twelve months prior to public announcement; and (2) acted on this information by purchasing the securities of positive change firms and selling short the securities of negative change firms. It is on the basis of these types of trading rules that Collins (1975) tested the importance of segment data.

Security trading rules were tested for a sample of 92 firms, 35 of which reported neither revenue nor earnings data on a segment basis prior to 1971 (the nondisclosure group). The remaining 57 reported some revenue data but no profit data by segment prior to 1971 (the partial disclosure group). For these firms, Collins used consolidated-based and segment-based earnings forecasting models to predict earnings twelve months prior to their announcements. The models enlisted to make the predictions were those used in Collins (1976a) and described above. Predictions were made for the three one-year periods ending in March 1969, 1970 and 1971.

If the earnings predicted by the segment models were

greater than those elicited from the consolidated models, the trading strategy tested required that the investor purchase the security (take a long position). Conversely, if the segment-based predictions were less than the consolidated-based, a short position was taken (the security was sold short). These trading rules were assumed to be executed twelve months prior to the earnings announcements for each security in the nondisclosure and partial disclosure groups for each of the three years. The abnormal returns that an investor would have received by following these strategies were then computed for each group for each month, for each of the three years and for the three years combined. Corresponding returns were computed for buy-and-hold strategies for comparisons. In these calculations, it was assumed that the investor places an equal dollar amount (takes an equal dollar short position) in each security for which the segment-based forecast was greater (less) than the consolidated-based forecast.

Because segment earnings data were not publicly available, at least in financial reports, for the sample firms before March 1971, and only became available in 1971 as a result of the SEC 10-K requirement that firms retroactively report them on a five-year historical basis, Collins was able to determine whether an investor could have outperformed the market had these data been reported. The reasoning was that if an investor had these data and if he had been able to use them in the specified models to predict correctly unexpected changes in earnings, he could have achieved abnormally large rates of return. Evidence that abnormal returns could have been realized would suggest that formal disclosure of the information would have been useful in the 1968–1970 period and, therefore, is generally desirable.

Collins found that the trading rule "strategies performed substantially better for the nondisclosure firms than for the partial disclosure firms," and he concluded:

> Based on this evidence, disclosure of segment *revenue* data apparently does make a difference. The results suggest that investors were able to utilize this data to anticipate, to a large extent, changes in earnings which otherwise would have been "unexpected" had they relied totally

on consolidated data. Thus, disclosure of segment revenue data, as a minimum is indicated [emphasis added] (p. 156).

The bases for these conclusions are not particularly strong. If Collins' entire thirty-six month period is considered, it is found that the trading rules strategies did not yield average abnormal returns significantly different from zero. However, it is indicated "that 1970 may have been somewhat atypical," and results for the combined 1968–1969 period do provide significance. Nevertheless, the exclusion of one-third of the original observations and the examination of the combined 1968 and 1969 period only weakens the strength of Collins' conclusions.

Even if we accept the fact that trading rules based on the difference between the segment-based predictions and the consolidated-based predictions were profitable, we must be careful about the conclusions drawn. First, it should be emphasized that because the tests with respect to partial disclosure firms were generally insignificant, this suggests, as in earlier studies, that the value of segment earnings data, once sales data are known, is, at a minimum, questionable. Also, returns to investors were not adjusted for transaction costs nor the cost of compiling data from external sources such as the *U.S. Industrial Outlook* or the SEC Statistical Series which were critical to the segment-based models.

4. Income Changes and the Timing of Market Reaction

As discussed in the foregoing section, Ball and Brown's study (1968) revealed that the market response to income numbers, as measured by security price adjustments, was relatively large in the twelve months prior to the announcement, relatively small in the month of the announcement, and negligible in the post-announcement months. The two studies reported on in this section directly relate (1) the availability of segment data to (2) the timing of security price adjustments to earnings. The question addressed is: Does the presence of historical segment data permit better forecasts of future earnings which, in turn, cause security prices to impound future earnings more quickly than if the data were not available? The underlying premise is that if security prices do respond more quickly to future earnings when segment data are disclosed, then disclosure is warranted. Investor decisions would benefit, leading to a more efficient allocation of resources in the economy.

In seeking to ascertain the effect of segment reporting, Kochanek (1974) classified firms with respect to voluntary segment disclosure in their annual reports prior to the SEC requirement. Based on a list of desirable content and format reporting characteristics, e.g., whether sales, assets and income were reported by segment and how clearly the information was presented, 37 firms were rated according to the quality of segment reporting for each of the four years between 1966 and 1969. These ratings served as a basis for classifying firms as "superior," "good," and "poor" reporters.

Next, the relationship between changes in annual income figures and changes in stock prices was measured for firms in each of the three groups using four Spearman rank correlations. The four correlations differed in that the reported income figures were correlated with changes in stock prices leading or lagging the reported income figures by different intervals. Specifically, yearly income figures were correlated with changes in security prices (1) 24–12 months before year end (long term); (2) 12–6 months before year end (intermediate term); (3) 6 months to year end (short term); and (4) year end to 3 months after (current). Kochanek hypothesized that good segment reporting enables more accurate and more distant forecasts of earnings and, therefore, security price adjustments to future earnings for good reporters should precede adjustments for poor reporters. If this is the case, he reasoned that the long term and intermediate term correlations should be stronger for good segment disclosers than for poor disclosers. With respect to the short term and current correlations, he predicted the opposite relationship, i.e., since investors would be less able to make distant earnings predictions for poor reporters, one would expect a greater response to income numbers close to and possibly even subsequent to year-end announcements.

Results of the Mann-Whitney U test at the .05 level of significance confirmed the *a priori* expectation that "good" reporters would exhibit higher positive Spearman rank correlation coefficients in the intermediate and long term models than "poor reporters" (p. 256). As hypothesized, he also found short term and current stock market reactions to earnings announcements stronger for poor reporters than for good reporters. However, "[s]imilar tests conducted between 'superior' and 'good' reporters failed to reject the null hypothesis of no difference at the .10 significance level in any of the four correlation models" (p. 256).

Kochanek also tested whether good reporters exhibited lower weekly stock fluctuations than poor reporters. The results of those tests were somewhat mixed when other explanatory variables such as growth, stability of earnings, and dividend policy were accounted for. Nevertheless, Kochanek concluded that segment data facilitate better earnings predictions and reduce uncertainty as measured by weekly security price variability.

As recognized by Kochanek and noted by Barefield and Comiskey (1975a), Kochanek's results were dependent on the reliability of the particular index developed to distinguish between good and poor reporters. Also, the results might have been sensitive to group characteristics other than segment reporting differences. Finally, Griffin and Nichols (1976, pp. 3-4) called attention to additional potential problems:

> [H]e fails to use the annual announcement data as a reference point; his price change ratio ignores the impact of cash dividend payments to stockholders; his "stock price change ratios" ignore important monthly return movements during the long term, intermediate term, etc., periods observed, and he is seemingly vague about describing the procedure used to adjust price changes for market movements.

Griffin and Nichols (1976) attempted to overcome the limitations which they perceived in a study which utilized a subset of Kochanek's sample. These authors tracked the behavior of unexpected monthly returns seventeen months prior to earnings announcements to six months after. Return adjustments during this period were viewed as a function of unexpected earnings changes which depended on the availability of segment disclosure. As in the previous work cited, it was hypothesized that disclosure will lead to less surprise and therefore less return adjustments in the period surrounding the earnings announcements.

Using a naive aggregate expectations model, Griffin and Nichols classified firms as having favorable or unfavorable unexpected earnings changes (expectation errors) based on the difference between actual earnings and the model's predictions. Cumulative average residuals were computed for positive and negative expectation errors.

An examination of these errors indicated that residuals for the poor reporters consistently exceeded residuals for the good reporters for the ten-month period prior to the announcement. Furthermore, for the four-month period after the time of the announcement, there was no evidence of any drift in the residuals for good reporters, while for the poor reporters a positive drift was detected. It was concluded "that the equilibrium values of firms that publicly disclose segment revenue and/or profit data may reflect agents' perceived changes in expected risk and return assessments at an earlier moment in time" (p. 7).

5. Impact of Segment Information on Security Risk and Return

In expressing support for segment disclosure, financial analysts claimed that such information is necessary to assess the sensitivity of company operations to circumstances in different industries and to changes in economy-wide conditions. These and other arguments reflect the recognition given to the importance of systematic risk (beta coefficients) in security valuation. Increasing recognition has been given to systematic risk since the evolution of capital market theory beginning with Sharpe (1964), Lintner (1965) and Mossin (1966) more than fifteen years ago.

A major implication of the theory is that the rates of return on individual securities and on portfolios depend not on the total risk or variability of a security but only on its systematic portion. The systematic portion, measured by the beta coefficient, reflects that part of return variability which results from the association between the asset's return and the return on the market as a whole.

Proponents of disclosure by segment have argued that disaggregated data are needed to properly evaluate future earnings and systematic risk for a diversified firm. When these data are first released, it is asserted, investors will reassess the systematic risk and value of securities on the basis of the new information. In particular, if it is discovered that a firm's performance is less (more) sensitive to economy-wide events than previously believed, investors would attribute less (more) risk to their invested capital and security prices would rise (fall). This process is viewed as bringing forth an improvement in the allocation of resources. Additionally, if updated information is available on a continuing basis, analysts will be able to detect shifts in emphasis among segments within diversified firms more quickly and accurately.

The link between segment information and the determination of systematic risk was more formally scrutinized by Collins and Simonds (1979). Reviewing and extending the results of Fama and Miller (1972, pp. 295–305) and Rubinstein (1973), they identified the mathematical relationship between the market risk of a firm and the proportion of the firm's resources committed to each of its product lines. This relationship was then used as a point of departure for explaining the usefulness of segment information.

Rubinstein (1973) had examined the relationship between a multi-activity firm's beta, its operating risk, and accounting variables such as fixed and variable costs per unit. As Collins and Simonds point out, the analysis by Rubinstein suggests that knowledge of the composition of a firm's portfolio of assets may be useful for risk evaluation. To the extent that segment sales and earnings information reflect this, knowledge of these variables may be equally useful. Also critical to the measurement of systematic risk are the firm's contribution margin (cash flows), influence (correlation) of economy-wide events on the output of product lines and "uncertainty of output per dollar of assets." To the extent that these variables, and therefore firm systematic risk, can be more accurately measured using segmented information, the securities markets will be more efficient if that information is made available to all market participants.

Progress toward deriving the relationship among segment accounting information, individual firm activities, and systematic risk is extremely important. Yet, it is merely suggestive of the potential value of segment data. It is not evidence of such. As pointed out by Ball and Brown (1969, p. 313), and recognized by Collins and Simonds, one may not be able to use segment information to obtain better estimates of critical variables:

[I]t is not clear that the market can gain a greater appreciation of the covariance of the firm [with the market] in total from an analysis of the individual covariances of the separate divisions rather than from a direct analysis of the covariance of the total earnings of the firm. One may well view this essentially empirical issue as the major relevant source of dispute in the external reporting of divisional performance.

Collins and Simonds recognized that because segment data may "suffer from severe contamination and/or measurement problems," they may be dysfunctional. Potential problems might be caused by poorly defined segments or inconsistent allocation of common costs. These concerns are well documented in the testimony on the measurement issue referred to previously.

With these considerations in mind, Collins and Simonds (1978, 1979) tested whether segment disclosure affects firm risk estimates. Specifically, the authors attempted to determine whether a shift in firm betas occurred during the time interval surrounding the period when line of business earnings data first were required by the SEC.

The methodology relied on was the ANCOVA or Chow test. This test required that beta coefficients be estimated (1) on the basis of data from the period before the event; (2) on the basis of data from the period after the event; and (3) on the basis of pooled data from before and after the event. Squared residuals (error terms) from applying regressions to before and after periods separately were compared to residuals from the pooled regressions. Large residual values for pooled regressions relative to values for separate regressions would be supportive of a shift in the risk coefficients.

This procedure was performed for a sample of treatment firms, i.e., those for which line of business data by segment were not available prior to 1971, and groups of multi-product and single-product control firms. The evidence presented supported the hypothesis that a significant systematic risk decline occurred for the treatment sample relative to the multi-and single-product control samples. The implication is that the disclosure of line of business profit data caused a reduction in systematic risk, i.e., returns to security holders were less responsive to general market movements.

Relying on a very different methodology, Dhaliwal (1978) provided evidence which is consistent with that reported by Collins and Simonds (1979). The objective of his study was to measure the impact of the 1970 line of business requirement on a firm's cost of capital. Three surrogates for a firm's cost of capital, namely, systematic risk, total risk, and a measure based on the dispersion parameter of the stable symmetric distribution, were regressed on several financial variables reflecting firm dividend policy, growth, size, leverage, liquidity and earnings variability, and one dummy variable. The dummy variable assumed a zero value for pre–1970 requirement observations and a value of one for post–1970 observations. Dhaliwal found that the coefficient of the dummy variable generally took a negative value in regressions for the treatment group which was composed of those firms which did not report segment data prior to 1971, and a positive value for the control group, which included firms that had reported on a segment basis as early as 1967. The signs of the dummy variable coefficients supported the hypothesis that there was a relative decline in the cost of capital (risk) for first-time segment disclosures.

The unsettling aspect of the Collins and Simonds and Dhaliwal studies is that there is little theory to explain the risk decline which was detected for firms first disclosing segment data. The theory reviewed above which relates operating risk, beta and the activities of multi-segment firms does suggest that segment disclosure, if unavailable elsewhere, may affect investors' risk estimates. However, it does not indicate that the beta shift necessarily would be in a negative direction. The additional disclosure might reveal that a firm's production activities and earnings variability are either more strongly or less strongly correlated with analogous market variables than earlier believed. Thus, even if we assume that data by segment provides useful information for systematic risk evaluation, there is no reason to expect that this evaluation would led to a risk decline. In fact, as detailed by Horwitz and Kolodny (1978, p. 660), the opposite result might be hypothesized:

> For, if the market were efficient and a firm recognized that reporting LOBUR profit data would have reduced its market risk, it would be inclined to voluntarily make that information public prior to the regu-

latory requirement in order to lower its cost of capital. Firms most likely to have withheld the information would be those for which disclosure would increase market risk and cause a greater cost of capital. Therefore, with the imposition of the requirement, one may have hypothesized an increase in the risk level for the treatment group (those firms which had not previously released the information).

The sole argument in support of the notion that risk would be reduced rests on the value of segment reporting for forecasting income. In particular, it has been maintained that risk reduction may follow the release of segment information because such data may improve forecasting ability. This reasoning assumes (1) that earnings predictions do in fact become more accurate; (2) that greater accuracy lessens the uncertainty associated with future earnings; and (3) that less uncertainty leads to less systematic risk.

Horwitz and Kolodny (1978) examined the adequacy of these assumptions. They observed that additional segment information may affect both the expected value and the variance associated with the distribution of a firm's future earnings. However, both parameters may increase or decrease with more complete information. Of immediate concern is the fact that the variance (risk) might increase if line of business "information revealed that the profitability of segments is more highly correlated than was earlier estimated or that the total operating risk of the firm was greater than earlier believed. In either case, after disclosure, the participant would estimate that there was more uncertainty associated with the earnings of the firm than before disclosure" (p. 660). Thus, one would not necessarily expect systematic risk reductions across all firms.

A second point on this matter relates to the evidence regarding forecasting accuracy presented in earlier studies, e.g., Kinney (1971), Collins (1976). Recall that these studies concluded that the availability of segment earnings data causes virtually no improvement in forecasts. Similarly, Barefield, Comiskey and Snyir (1979) found no evidence of a reduction in the average prediction errors of, or the consensus among, analysts contingent on segment earnings information. It is the effect of segment earnings data on risk reduction which Collins and Simonds and Dhaliwal explored. Thus, an underlying assumption of these studies, i.e., that forecasting accuracy improves, appears to be inconsistent with existing evidence.

Research by Horwitz and Kolodny (1977) also considered the impact of line of business profit disclosure required as of 1971. The objective of the first part of a two-part study was similar to that of Collins and Simonds and Dhaliwal: to ascertain whether the release of segment profit data prompted investors to reevaluate security risk. The second part analyzed market model residuals to determine whether security prices were adjusted to impound other changes in expectations prompted by the new information, such as changes in expected cash flows.

To measure risk changes, absolute values of changes in betas from predisclosure to post-disclosure periods were computed for two samples of firms: a group of firms which were required to report on a product-line basis for the first time in 1971 (experimental sample) and a single-product control sample. The computed values were averaged for each of the two groups and statistically compared. The reason for calculating the absolute value of changes was that, as noted earlier, there is no theory to suggest that, if the data did affect risk perceptions, the effect would be consistently positive or negative across firms. The difference in means test indicated no significant difference between the beta changes observed for the two groups.

Collins and Simonds (1978) criticized this aspect of the Horwitz and Kolodny study in two respects. First, they contended that the results may have been biased because firms included in the treatment group might have disclosed segment data between July 1969 and January 1971 in registration and proxy statements. If such information had been previously available, no reaction to the information would have been expected in 1971. Checks of the sample later revealed that only three of the fifty treatment firms filed such statements. The other criticism was levied at the methodology that Horwitz and Kolodny used to test for beta shifts. As Collins and Simonds indicated, the tests may have been insufficiently strong to detect some beta shifts.

In the second part of Horwitz and Kolodny's study, monthly return residuals, absolute values of monthly return residuals, cumulative average residuals, and cumulative average absolute residuals were calculated for the period surrounding the release of the segment data. Residuals were used to measure changes in expectations regarding future firm performance. Cumulative residuals were examined to identify effects which occurred gradually over a period greater than one month. The absolute value statistics were tracked because there was no evidence that the effect of segment information, if present, would be in the form of abnormal price increases or abnormal price decreases. Assuming that investors, in reacting to new information, bid up the prices for some securities and sold off other securities, positive and negative return residuals would have offset each other had not absolute values been taken.

The monthly sets of residuals and returns for the two groups were subjected to both market model and other tests. No significant differences in the behavior of the security prices were found either over time for the treatment group or between the treatment and control groups. Hence, these results did not support the premise that the disclosure of segment income data furnished investors with valuable information.

The conclusions resulting from the foregoing review of the empirical studies are summarized in section E. Briefly, however, it is evident that the research to date indicates the need for and the usefulness of segmented revenue data. However, little if any evidence exists today which supports the usefulness of earnings reporting by segment or any of the additional requirements set forth under FAS 14 and SEC Regulation S-K.

How, then, can one explain the initiation of segment profit reporting in 1969 and its subsequent development to S-K? As hypothesized in the next section, it may be a manifestation of a change in the balance of financial regulation between the FASB and the SEC.

D. PUBLIC VERSUS PRIVATE STANDARD SETTING

The SEC, unlike the FASB, is not dependent upon private funds for its survival, and it has manifested less patience with evaluating change before taking additional steps. This was true initially when the APB desired to wait to see how voluntary segment disclosures would work, and it was true recently when the SEC was unwilling to evaluate the results of Statement No. 14 before issuing new rules in its Regulation S–K which went beyond No. 14.

It may be that the consequences of increased disclosure is not the real issue, although the language of cost versus benefit is frequently used. As we have summarized in the preceding section, the empirical research cannot be used to support the appropriateness of segment profit reporting. What may be relevant here, as we indicated in section B, is the general movement toward "corporate democracy," and the perception that increased disclosure is, like sunshine, the best disinfectant and just as free.

It is not clear whether segment earnings reporting helps investors by providing useful information or whether it simply advances government policy generally. One difficulty is that there is no correcting mechanism that will cause the SEC to reduce those disclosure requirements which have little benefit but significant cost associated with their production and dissemination. On the contrary, the SEC, like other regulatory agencies in similar circumstances, has increased the details of segment reporting requirements when it appeared that the benefits were too small. The latter is presumed to have resulted from requirements which were too broad.

One measure of the trend toward increased disclosure, of which segment profit reporting is only one example, is the secular increase in the size of Form 10–K. In the ten-year period, 1968–1978, the 10–K manifested double digit growth. For NYSE companies the average number of pages in 1968 was 56, including exhibits, and in 1978 the average number of pages, including exhibits, was 165. This represents an annual growth rate of 12 percent.

Perhaps, like other public agencies, the SEC will usually err on the side of excess. The reason may lie in the nature of a bureaucracy and the functioning of an agency. Public agencies generally avoid risk and do not internalize the costs they impose. As long as it cannot be shown that harmful effects may ensue, or that a rule may be neutral, regulatory requirements will generally increase.

The SEC has shown that it is flexible where research indicates possible negative effects of a rule. This was true in the oil and gas decision where the SEC, in spite of its drive toward uniformity in measurement, revoked Statement No. 19 and allowed the continued use of nonuniform methods. This action followed evidence about negative economic effects (Collins and Dent, 1979) and lobbying against the expense-only ("successful efforts") rule.

Segment profit reporting, however, as indicated earlier, has only been tested for possible benefits. Evaluations have not been made about possible competitive harm. Thus, although the benefits of segment reporting have been found to be questionable, no anticompetitive harm has been found, so the costs have been ignored and disclosure has been mandated. The SEC may believe that for segment profit disclosure the costs will be internalized by all firms to no single firm's disadvantage. In other words, disclosure will be imposed when no external competitive harm can be forecast or determined, regardless of some increase in the reporting costs associated with compliance. When, however, possible harm is forecast or determined, such as in the case of the oil and gas rule, a requirement will likely not be imposed regardless of the alleged, but unmeasurable, benefits, such as "confidence" and "fairness."

One of the costs associated with segment profit reporting which has not been fully evaluated is the impact in the U.S. capital markets of U.S. companies being required to report segment earnings when foreign companies report only segment revenues. At the present time no foreign law or stock exchange rule mandates public disclosure of profits attributable to industry or geographic segments. The Fourth Directive on Company Law of the European Economic Community covering nine member states requires only a breakdown of sales revenue by product line and geographical area (Handbook, 1979).

The Securities and Exchange Commission, considering the need to have foreign issuers conform to U.S. requirements, accepted the contention of foreign companies that segment earnings reporting would result in too great a cost burden and would cause them competitive harm. The SEC was thus led to require only segment revenue data on its Form 20–F. It is not clear how the SEC determined that for foreign issuers mandating segment profits was cost inefficient but for U.S. issuers it was cost efficient.

More directly, if segment profit reporting is so important, as the SEC has argued for the last 10 years, does not the "secrecy" by foreign firms, which increasingly are raising capital in the U.S. equity market, place those firms in a more favorable position? If so, does it have economic consequences, i.e., is it "anticompetitive," a term used by the SEC in its 1975 amendment to the Securities Act of 1934? Also, and perhaps equally important, does it accord with the Commission's notion of "fairness"?

In sum, many issues associated with segment reporting have been raised. They encompass the basic problems of financial reporting, i.e., measurement, disclosure and auditing. The only regulations that can be compared with segment reporting in terms of their implications and comprehensiveness are the Securities Acts of 1933 and 1934 which first mandated accounting disclosure and assigned responsibility to the SEC for establishing disclosure and measurement rules for financial statements as a whole. The justification for those Acts, besides investor protection, has rested on its contribution to the increase in capital market efficiency (Burton, 1975). The drive to mandate segment reporting was supported by the same justification; in particular, by arguments that the ability of investors and creditors to evaluate the earnings potential and risk of diversified firms would be enhanced.

With respect to segment earnings reporting, which in many respects has been the focal point of all major disclosure and measurement requirements during the last decade, the research performed thus far indicates that its economic value is questionable. The analysis presented in this chapter may lead one to conclude that the explanation for mandating that profits be reported by segment cannot be sought in economic analysis alone but must be examined in the light of models that attempt to explain the behavior of public agencies.

E. SUMMARY AND CONCLUDING REMARKS

Two factors were particularly important in the history of segment reporting. The first factor was the growth of certain new types of corporations, the diversified conglomerate and the multinational corporation. Controversial themselves as efficient forms of organization, they seemed to create demands for different types of financial information for users. Secondly, an increased emphasis was placed upon the legal notion of "fairness," a belief that conditions should be created to eliminate (or limit) the advantages of "inside" information, thereby increasing the confidence of the public in the securities market. If segment information was useful to "insiders" and large investors, the "fairness" doctrine asserted that everyone should have access to it.

During the 1970s the major segment reporting rules were the FASB's statement No. 14 in 1976 and the SEC's Regulation S-K in 1978. Although adopting No. 14 in its S-K requirement, we have seen that the SEC went beyond it in several important respects without waiting a reasonable period to evaluate the effects of No. 14. The additional requirements of S-K may be summarized as follows:

1. The S-K required disclosure of the effect of market prices in inter-segment transfers when the basis used for transfer pricing is "substantially higher or lower than those charged to or received from unaffiliated parties . . . [and] is material to an understanding of the segment information."
2. The S-K required further segmentation of product class within each industry segment.
3. The S-K required the identity of major customers.
4. The S-K required 5 years of retroactive application; No. 14 stated that prospective application was sufficient.

With respect to the benefits of segment information, we have seen that proponents of such disclosure have claimed that the information is important for the evaluation of the earnings potential and risk of diversified firms. The need to test these claims led to the empirical research reviewed in the third section of this chapter. The central question examined by researchers was: What effect does the knowledge of segment information have on the value and risk of securities as perceived by investors? If segment information does not affect investor decisions, it must be justified on the grounds of providing some other benefit. Subject to the limitations cited earlier and at some cost of generalization, let us summarize the empirical results.

The research conducted on the use of forecasting models indicated that segment sales data can be utilized to improve earnings forecasts and to make better investment decisions, but that the availability of segment earnings numbers provides no marginal benefit. Secondly, when actual analysts' forecasts were examined, it was found that their predictions were no more accurate subsequent to required disclosure of segment earnings than before.

The direct studies based on security price adjustments yielded mixed results. It was found that the securities of firms which voluntarily disclosed more segment data in their annual reports in the late 1960s generally were subject to less abnormal returns around reporting time, and that earnings information seemed to be impounded in the security prices of these firms earlier than for firms which provided little or no segment data. With respect to the effect of the SEC disclosure law pertaining to line of business reporting, the evidence is unclear. Although not consistent across all studies, there is some indication that a reduction in perceived risk was associated with the requirement. Yet, the examinations of abnormal returns did not indicate that the capital market received any unanticipated information relevant to valuation when segment earnings data were first disclosed.

Looking to future research, given that No. 14 and S-K are in place, there exists a need to assess their possible benefits. In doing so, it seems that the analysis might first be limited to those companies which have provided large amounts of incremental information on segments. For example, this analysis could be limited to those companies that increased disclosure from only the company as a whole to seven or eight segments. Otherwise, if no benefits were found for the set of all companies increasing segment disclosure, it always could be argued by advocates of segment reporting that the rules were too lax and that greater 'fineness" of segments should be demanded.

In addition to gathering further evidence concerning the possible beneficial effects of "more complete" segment reporting, also it is important that estimates be gathered on the costs of that disclosure; for evidence that security prices are affected by the formal release of segment data does not necessarily imply that they have social value. To reach this conclusion, we require a method of converting affected security price changes into a metric that can be used for comparison with the cost of preparing such data. To demonstrate that potential benefits result from additional disclosure is no longer adequate without consideration of related costs. This task remains unresolved at present.

One final observation deserves attention. It should be emphasized that any existing evidence that security prices are not affected by the formal release of additional segment data, either in annual reports or 10-K's, voluntarily or involuntarily, does not necessarily imply that those data are of no value. If segment data are important, they may be available to market participants through channels other than financial statements. In such a case, they may be impounded in security prices well before they appear on annual reports or 10-K's.

NOTES

1. Scherer's discussion relates to the desire of the FTC for segmented sales information, and Sweden is cited as an example of a government which publicly discloses "sales segmented by industry for single enterprises." In correspondence with the authors, however, he indicated that this was not accurate. Specifically, the Swedish Central Statistical Office does not publish such data, and they may be made available to scholars only after permission from affected firms. Sweden, like all countries except the U.S., does not require publication of segment earnings data from firms. For an opposite point of view, i.e., that the corporation is a voluntary association created by contract, see Hessen (1979).

2. Voluntary segment reporting of sales revenue was much more common during this period. For instance in 1968, 318 companies out of 600 reported segment revenue, and by 1974 the number increased to 515 (Twombly, 1978).

3. An example of product class is given in ASR 224: A chemical company could have a chemical/metals segment which includes inorganic chemicals, metals, and functional products. Analysts had previously asserted the need for product class information in order to determine market share.

4. This generalization based on averages should not hide the fact that the range of the number of segments included companies with one segment and a few with segments as high as ten. Ernst & Ernst shows no companies out of its sample of 126 with segments greater than 8. Arthur Andersen shows only 3 companies out of 250 with segments above 8 with a maximum of 10, the limitation stated in No. 14.

5. Regulation S-K does require the identity of the segment but not the dollar amount of R & D when the outlays are considered to be material.

6. This assumption will be discussed further (Section C.2) after reviewing the literature.

Appendix V.1. Selected Issues in the Development of Segment Reporting

Issue	SEC-LOB (Unaudited) Effective 1–1–1970	Exposure Draft Prior To FAS 14	FAS 14 Effective 12–15–1976	SEC S–K Effective 3–15–1978
1. Segment Definition	Rate of profitability, degree of risk and opportunities for growth are guides for segmentation. Revenue and pretax earnings before extraordinary items must be at least 10 percent of related combined totals. Upper limit of 10 segments. Disclosure of product class revenue from sales to unaffiliated customers.	Three digit industry SIC code to serve as a guide, but determination on the basis of management's judgment. Revenue, operating profit, or identifiable assets must be 10 percent or more of its related total combined revenue (including intersegment revenue), combined operating profit, and combined identifiable assets. Upper limit of 10 segments.	Same.	Same, except within each industry segment a further segment of product class for sales to unaffiliated customers.

2. Intersegment and Intraenterprise Transfer	Disclosure of method and effects if it materially affects the reported contribution to income.	Transfers accounted at prices that "realistically determine operating profit." If change is made, the effect on profit and loss and the justification, with a statement of preferability, should be disclosed.	Basis always disclosed. Transfers accounted for by basis actually used internally.	Same as No. 14, except basis disclosed only when transfer prices are substantially higher or lower than market prices, and where such a difference is material to an understanding of segment information. In such a case, the effect on segment revenue and profit should be disclosed.
3. Level of Reported Profit for Segment	Pretax earnings.	Profit and loss contribution and operating profit or loss.	Operating profit or loss.	Same as No. 14.
4. Common Cost Allocation, Excluding Central Administrative Costs	Disclosure only if it materially affects reported contribution to income.	Allocation on "a reasonable basis."	Same	Same

(*continued*)

Appendix V.1—(Continued)

Issue	SEC-LOB (*Unaudited*) *Effective 1-1-1970*	Exposure Draft Prior To FAS 14	FAS 14 *Effective 12-15-1976*	SEC S-K *Effective 3-15-1978*
5. Identifiable Assets of Segment	None	Used exclusively by segment plus portion of joint assets allocated "on a reasonable basis."	Same	Same
6. Retroactivity	5 years	Not required.	Not required.	3 years of revenue, profit or loss, and identifiable assets. Previous line of business data may be used if filed, with lack of comparability of segments explained.
7. Major Customers	Name of customer if loss of which would have a material adverse effect.	The name and importance disclosed, but no guide is stated for disclosure.	Disclosure if at least ten percent of total revenue is derived from a single customer or group of customers. Customer need not be named.	Same, but customer must be named.

8. Foreign Operations	Disclosure only when there is a material amount of revenue. In such a case, relative profitability should be disclosed. Geographic basis not used, only volume of foreign sales.	Stress on degrees of risk, profitability, and growth in different countries or groups of countries. No quantitative guides.	Stress on foreign and domestic operations. Foreign revenue or identifiable assets must be at least 10 percent of respective firm's totals. Can be disaggregated into geographic area where the 10 percent minimum (above) is satisfied.	Same
9. Interim reporting	Not required.	Required if a complete set of interim financial statements is issued.	Same, but later suspended by FASB Statement No. 18.	Not required.
10. Research and Development Costs	Not required.	Required if significant and important to an understanding of the segment.	Not required.	Only the identity of the segment if the amount is material.

Controversy and Evidence With Respect to the Economic Consequences of Particular Measurement Rules

This chapter reviews the issues and evidence concerning the alleged consequences of measurement rules pertaining to the investment tax credit, self-insurance reserves, developing stage companies, foreign currency translation and exploration and development costs. Also examined is a Department of Commerce study on the economic effects of FAS 2 on R & D.

A. THE INVESTMENT TAX CREDIT

The Investment Tax Credit (ITC) first became effective in 1962. The ITC allowed an immediate reduction in a firm's federal tax liability of seven percent of the cost of investment in qualified assets. At that time, the method of reporting the tax reduction came under study by the Accounting Principles Board (APB). The Board considered which one of the two reporting methods, flow-through or deferral, best reflected economic activity and, therefore, should be used in financial reporting.

The use of flow-through or deferral could lead to significantly different results being reported in a firm's financial statements. Like deferral, flow-through reduces the income tax liability to the government. Unlike deferral, however, flow-through permits the tax reduction to be taken entirely into the current year's income statement and thus causes a greater immediate increase in profit. Because deferral results in the tax benefit being recognized in the income statement over the entire life of the asset, in the year of the investment the increase in profit due to the ITC is less than that for flow-through when the firm is growing.

The APB studied the question after the submission of opinions by the Big Eight accounting firms which were evenly split on the issue. It concluded in Opinion 2 that the ITC was equivalent to a reduction of the costs of the assets, that income cannot arise from the acquisition of assets, and therefore, that ". . . spreading the income in some rational manner over a series of future accounting periods is more logical and supportable." Consequently, it ruled that the deferral method must be used.

The reaction to APB 2 was immediate. The Opinion was passed in December 1962 and the SEC issued ASR 96 in January 1963. That release effectively revoked APB 2 because there had been "substantial diversity of opinion among responsible persons in the matter of accounting for the investment credit." The Commission stated in the Release that it would accept financial statements under the Exchange Acts using either the flow-through or the deferral method. Several months later, in March 1964, the Board, stating that its opinions rested "upon their general acceptability," issued APB 4 which revoked APB 2 and allowed both methods to continue to be used.

Apparently, a significant number of corporate managements expressed to the SEC their desire to use flow-through on the grounds that it, rather than deferral, was more in accordance with the purpose of the ITC, the stimulation of investment. That is, it was believed that the use of flow-through by permitting the recognition of more accounting profit, even though the ex-ante cash flows would be the same under either method, would be itself a causal factor in stimulating more investment.

A similar controversy was generated in 1971 when the investment tax credit (then called the Job Development Credit) was reinstated. While discussion was taking place as to whether the APB should evaluate the methods once more, Congress added an amendment to the new law which specifically allowed firms to select either method of measurement. The proposal for an amendment covering the measurement question was supported by the Treasury Department. In a letter to Senator Long, Chairman of the Senate Finance Committee, the Acting Secretary of the Treasury, Charles Walker stated that "The vast majority of the companies have followed the former alternative [flow-through]—reflecting the benefit of the credit immediately in earnings. It seems self-evident that these businessmen will have less motivation to purchase new equipment if the benefits of the credit are not reflected in operating results when realized...." (Department of the Treasury, 1971). The evidence supporting such a contention was not forthcoming, and 8 years later, when the issue arose again, the Deputy Assistant Secretary (Tax Analysis) of the Treasury Department stated that "regardless of how the subsidy [ITC] is presented in an unregulated company's financial books of account, market prices and output will respond to the real underlying change in private costs. Prices and costs are equilibrated in unregulated markets independently of accounting formalities" (Department of the Treasury, 1979).

Because a single method of measuring the investment tax savings was never mandated for unregulated companies, it has been impossible to determine what the economic effects on companies would have been if they were forced to use a single method.

B. MEASUREMENT OF LOSS CONTINGENCIES

In FAS 5, "Accounting for Contingencies," the FASB established criteria for the measurement of a contingency. A contingency was defined as:

> "...an existing condition, situation, or set of circumstances involving uncertainty as to possible gain ... or loss ... to an enterprise that will ultimately be resolved when one or more future events occur or fail to occur. Resolution of the uncertainty may confirm the acquisition of an asset or the reduction of a liability or the loss or impairment of an asset or the incurrence of a liability" (FAS 5, par. 1).

The statement focused on loss contingencies—incurrences of a liability or the impairment of an asset.

Examples of loss contingencies were, among others, the risk of loss or damage to a company's property by fire and the risk of loss from catastrophes that is assumed by property and casualty insurance companies. The two basic measurement problems were: (1) the determination of the period in which the loss should be recognized; and (2) the determination of the amount to be recorded before the exact amount of the loss is known.

A number of property and casualty insurance companies had adopted, prior to FAS 5, a policy of making a provision from each period's income to cover a portion of major losses expected to occur in the future. In addition, some companies which were self-insured (i.e., uninsured) accrued losses periodically based upon some expectation about the size and timing of expected future occurrences of large property losses. The creation of such self-insured "reserves" reduced profit and sometimes, because of the uncertainty about both the actual size and time of the loss, were placed on corporate balance sheets between the liabilities and stockholders' equity sections.

FAS 5, by tightening the criteria for loss recognition, eliminated self-insurance reserves and, in the case of insurance companies, catastrophe reserves. At the time of the hearings, some interested parties argued that the Statement, by eliminating the ability of companies to spread large, sporadic losses among many periods, would adversely affect the economic decisions of affected firms. Many firms, it was contended, would be forced to purchase insurance or reinsurance because the "protection" of the accrual had been removed.

Such a contention seems to have been based upon two assumptions. First, management desires to smooth or normalize income. Second, when measurement methods are eliminated that achieve this goal, management will use real expenditures to reduce volatility in the belief that the firm will be less worse off from the use of uneconomic outlays than from the increase in the volatility of its income stream.

The only test conducted to determine whether affected firms did, in fact, alter their real outlays for insurance was a survey study. The difficulty of gaining access to data on insurance expenditures precluded the use of an empirical study. The analysis of survey responses of corporations using self-insurance reserves prior to FAS 5 led to the conclusion that there was no significant change in the pattern of expenditures associated with insurance of affected firms as compared to a sample of control firms (Goshay, 1978). Thus, the evidence supported the position that FAS 5 did not encourage risk and insurance managers to purchase insurance on uncovered exposures that was not economically justified.

C. MEASUREMENT BY DEVELOPING STAGE ENTERPRISES

The question of the potential economic impact on the choice between deferral and expense appeared again in FAS 7, *Accounting and Reporting by Development Stage Enterprises*. The problem addressed here was whether firms in the start-up or development stage could defer their pre-operating costs or whether these costs had to be expensed. The Board adopted the expense position on the grounds that these firms should use the same measurement principles as operating firms. When the certainty of recoverability of pre-operating costs is low, which is the typical case, the Board required expensing. In this Statement the Board reported the concern by some respondents that the rule, requiring development stage companies to use the same generally accepted accounting principles as established companies, would make it difficult, if not impossible, to obtain capital. "They suggested that those requirements would likely cause many development stage enterprises to report periodic losses in an income statement. . . . Because those results would not be fully understood, suppliers of capital would be disinclined to invest in these enterprises" (FAS 7, par. 48).

The Board cited interview evidence to oppose this contention (FAS 7, par. 49). Yet earlier in the Statement (par. 38) it asserted, without providing even interview evidence, that deferral of pre-operating costs, recommended by the American Institute of Certitifed Public Accountants, would have likely "fooled" users by inflating assets.

The Board believes . . . that the distinction between costs that would be reported as "assets" and costs that would be reported as "unrecovered costs" or "cumulative cost outlays" [deferred costs] under the SEC and AICPA Committee approaches is one that is likely to be overlooked by many financial statement users . . . the nature of development-stage activities and their related costs can best be indicated by... disclosures ... rather than by accumulation or deferral of costs that would be charged to expense when incurred, if generally accepted accounting principles ... were applied (FAS 7, par. 38).

Thus, it appears that the Board believed that supplementary disclosure when the expense method is used is more useful than the deferral method with supplementary disclosure.

D. MEASUREMENT OF FOREIGN CURRENCY TRANSLATIONS

Financial Accounting Standards Board Statement 8 on foreign currency translations is another area which has generated controversy about its alleged negative economic effects. Statement 8, which became effective in January 1976, established a single set of rules for U.S. multinational companies to use when translating foreign currency transactions, assets, and liabilities into U.S. dollars for financial reporting purposes. Before that date several methods could be used, although two alternatives, current-noncurrent or monetary-nonmonetary, were the most widely practiced.

The statement contained two provisions that could have produced significant changes in reported profit:

1. All foreign exchange gains and losses, whether realized or unrealized, were required to be closed to the Profit and Loss Statement. Many critics contended that such a requirement would increase the volatility of reported profit.
2. When a foreign exchange rate changed, assets valued in the foreign currency, such as property, plant, equipment and inventories, were not to be revalued in U.S. dollars. Multinationals continued to use the historic (original) cost principle for these items. Liabilities in foreign debt, however, were to be valued using the current or most recent exchange rate.

The second provision related to the method required by the statement, known as the temporal method. Some critics argued that this method leads to an important inconsistency. Foreign operations typically are exposed economically in a net asset position, but the temporal method requires fixed assets and most inventory to be translated at historical rates while measuring liabilities abroad at current rates. This leads to an accounting exposure of a net liability position. Consequently, exhange gains or losses which are reported may result in interpretations which are not implied by the economic results.

Although criticism has been strong, and a revision of No. 8 is likely which purportedly will lead to the use of current exchange rates for all balance sheet items plus removal of exchange gains or losses from earnings to stockholders' equity, research on this issue has not indicated that No. 8 had significant economic effects. The empirical work has concentrated on the effects of No. 8 on foreign exchange risk practices by means of a questionnaire study of corporate officials (Evans, et al., 1978) and by an analysis of changes in hedging practices by multinationals after No. 8 became effective (U.S. Treasury, 1978). Both studies were unable to conclude that, on the average, any altered practices in either financing, investment or hedging activities adversely impacted the cash flow positions of affected companies.

Studies addressed to the possible security market effects of mandating the temporal method showed that FAS 8 had no significant effect on the stock market values of affected multinationals. Dukes (1978) and (Shank, et al., 1978) found that the rule had no measurable effect on security returns at the five percent significance level.

Subsequent research by Griffin (1980) examined the responses of critics to FAS 8 following a post-enactment evaluation of FAS 1–12. The results of his study are of particular interest because of their relevance to two other Statements discussed later, FAS 19 on oil and gas accounting and FAS 2 on the measurement of R & D investment expenditures. Analyzing a sample of 119 firms which submitted letters to the Board concerning FAS 8 and a second sample of 479 multinationals which did not, Griffin determined that the rule had a relatively minor impact on the annual and quarterly earnings of the average multinational. Moreover, there did not appear to be a statistically significant difference between the two samples in either the median of the absolute value of exchange gains and losses or in measures of variability of those exchange gains or losses (either annually or quarterly). The average ratio of the exchange gain or loss to quarterly pre-tax net income was approximately nine percent for 1976 and 1977; the average annual ratios for those years was about six percent. The effect of the rule thus appeared to be relatively small on the average.

In the remainder of the study, Griffin used multivariate logit analysis to select significant discriminating variables which would predict whether multinationals submitted critical letters to the Board. Using a number of explanatory variables, including the exchange gain or loss ratio, his results indicated that only two variables had discriminatory power: size and leverage.

E. MEASUREMENT OF UNSUCCESSFUL ACTIVITY BY OIL AND GAS COMPANIES

Prior to December 1978, companies in the oil and gas industry could select among two rules to measure the expenditures for drilling and exploration activities of unsuccessful efforts (dry holes)—the successful efforts costing method (SE) and the full costing method (FC).

A single, uniform method was sought because the Energy Policy and Conservation Act of 1975 directed the SEC to assure the development and observance of accounting practices that would enable the Department of Energy to obtain information necessary for a reliable energy data base. The SEC turned to the FASB to study the question and to determine the single, most appropriate method.

The FASB effort, which commenced in 1975, resulted in the issuance of FAS 19, *Financial Accounting and Reporting by Oil and Gas Producing Companies,* in December 1977. The Statement required all companies to use SE, the method that required outlays on unsuccessful efforts to be fully expensed (charged against current revenues) instead of deferred (amortized over time together with outlays which led to successful activity).

The controversy which followed the issuance of FAS 19 involved one of the most challenging tests of the 1938 decision (reaffirmed in 1973) of the SEC to allow the accounting standard-setting function to operate in the private sector, subject to SEC oversight. The chairman of the FASB, D. Kirk, stated that ". . . the Commission's decision on Statement No. 19

could prove to be the most important decision concerning private sector standard setting since the 3–2 Commission vote in 1937 [sic] that set the policy of looking to the private sector for leadership in the establishment of accounting principles" (Kirk, 1978).

The SEC, having responsibility for measurement rules under the 1934 Act given to it by Congress, was required to conduct hearings on FAS 19 because of a June 4, 1975 Amendment to the SEC 1934 Act which mandated that the SEC consider the impact of its own rules on competitive behavior. Under this amendment if the Commission determined that some burden on competition was necessary or appropriate, it had to include in its rulings a statement supporting such a determination.

The SEC hearings brought out different views about the nature of profit and assets. Some argued that exploration costs should be judged on the basis of the activity of a single well, and others contended that these costs should be considered as a portfolio and thus are related to the activities of all wells (successful and unsuccessful). Some asserted that deferral provides the appropriate income signal for its previous pattern of exploration and drilling activity; others contended that deferral disguises risk and that the function of accounting is to reveal risk.

The most important question, however, was whether the expensing requirement had an anticompetitive effect, the burden of proof resting on the SEC. The "proof" rested on the SEC because it was required to show either that there were no anticompetitive effects or that the "burden on competition [was] necessary or appropriate" in the furtherance of the SEC Acts. If it were established that there were no anticompetitive effects, then it would be easier to support the conclusions of FAS 19, both from the point of view of the advantages of uniformity and the alleged superiority of expensing (SE) over deferral (FC).

Testimony at the hearings raised serious doubts about the neutrality of the mandated rule on companies that previously had used full costing, all of which were small independent or subsidiary companies. The managements of several of these companies, as well as many consulting firms and investment bankers, asserted that firms forced to switch from FC to SE might reduce exploration and drilling costs. It was hypothesized that this action might be taken because the SE method could be used to manipulate income more easily, and cutting back on exploration and drilling would prevent what would otherwise be a sharp decline in profits for firms forced to switch methods. Some explained the decline in security returns of full cost companies found by Collins and Dent (1979) and in one part of Dyckman's study (1979) as an anticipation by the market of reductions in exploration activity. A typical statement coming from an investment banker was:

> It is our contention that this [mandated switch to successful efforts] will adversely affect investors' appraisal of these companies; this in turn will impair the companies' access to the equity capital markets and finally reduce and concentrate the exploration function as smaller independent companies either withdraw from this high-risk effort or merge with larger entities more able to absorb the earnings fluctuations (Chastly, 1978).

At related hearings held at the Department of Energy, another witness, the president of an independent natural resource company primarily in oil and gas exploration and production, asserted that:

> ... if we are forced to make this change [switch from full-cost to successful-efforts] we will reduce the dollar magnitude of our domestic petroleum exploration effort. We have not yet determined the exact amount of this reduction, but it will be significant. In determining future exploration strategy, investment decisions will be judged not simply on economic merit and exploration risk, but also on the "false" criteria of short term earnings' impact. We also probably will revise the nature of the balance of our exploration effort to reduce participation in high risk situations. ... We will seek out lower risk opportunities [Commons, undated].

Other managements of small, independent oil and gas companies appearing as witnesses before the agencies evaluating FAS 19 expressed similar positions, suggesting that a likely decline in exploration outlays would result from managements' belief that otherwise the firms would be adversely affected in the securities market. With respect to the equity market, it was claimed that underwriters might find it more difficult to market new issues and that additional time and effort would be required to explain to prospective buyers the reasons for the decline in profit, assets and net worth. Also, because of such declines, some believed that additional burdens in the debt market would be imposed, particularly for public debt. This perception was based, in part, on the fact that the provisions in bond indentures that define debt capacity and set limits on dividend payments are related to accounting variables, and thus a mandated change that reduces those variables will immediately affect the firms' debt capacity and ability to pay dividends to stockholders. This is discussed further in Chapter IV.

Other groups and agencies, including the Antitrust Division of the Justice Department, the Federal Energy Administration and the Federal Trade Commission, expressed reservations about the ruling, suggesting that negative economic consequences might ensue. For example, at the hearings before the SEC, the FTC testified that: "A firm delaying certain activities, will be able to alter its accounting earnings, and meet a perceived need to maintain high net income. Thus, an accounting change could lead to altered spending activity in a way that otherwise does not make good business or economic sense" (Federal Trade Commission, 1978, p. 27).

Evidence also was provided on this issue in a study of security market returns. In their research on FAS 19, Collins and Dent (1979) presented statistical evidence that the proposed mandated use of successful efforts was associated with a relative negative shift in returns for full cost firms when compared to those for successful efforts firms. This difference was found to last over an eight-month period from the time the July 15, 1977 Exposure Draft preceding FAS 19 was released through the issuance of the 1977 10–K and annual reports.

Collins and Dent explained their conclusions, at variance with previous research on the efficient market effect of alternative reporting methods involving no tax changes, by noting that previous research on this question had not fully encompassed the entire range of possibilities. Specifically, they suggested that previous research on switches in measurement techniques may not have detected relative negative returns because that research had been limited to voluntary changes in accounting methods that had increased reported earnings (Collins and Dent, 1979, pp. 7–8). Moreover, they pointed out that much of the previous efficient markets research had been confined to larger companies. Testimony at the oil and gas hearings revealed that most of the affected companies were small independent or subsidiary companies.

The FASB did not agree with the testimony that supported the premise that FAS 19 would have a negative impact on the exploration activities of full-cost companies. It agreed, of course, that the mandated change to successful efforts would reduce, perhaps significantly, profit, retained earnings and assets of affected firms. However, the evidence it gathered (the Dyckman study [1979] plus interviews) supported its contention that investors, lenders, and other suppliers of capital make their decisions on the basis of prospective cash flows that are unaffected by a switch in reporting techniques.

The Board also recognized the strong concern expressed by critics of the SE method regarding the increased volatility of earnings which would result from No. 19. The same issue had appeared in a number of projects considered by the Board where the object was also to mandate a single, uniform rule. The Board's judgment about this issue as it applied to the SE method in the oil and gas industry was the same as it was for the other projects: Fluctuating earnings is a characteristic not a fault, and investors and lenders are better able to evaluate the impact of risks by eliminating the deferral method.[1] As Chairman Kirk said:

> To be useful for informed investment decision making, earnings should reflect differences in risk, not obscure them. Smoothing to portray varying individual perceptions of "true earnings" or "potential earnings" obscures risk. In the Board's judgment, accounting standards should not be designed to take the peaks and valleys out of a high risk business . . . (Kirk, 1978).

The Board was willing to admit that its assertion of no harmful economic effects for affected firms could be wrong, but only for the short-run. It asserted that net social benefits would be greater even though some firms might be worse off, thus implying that FAS 19 would improve the allocation of resources to and within the oil and gas industry. "[I]n situations in which accounting changes may have had a long-term effect on security prices (as opposed to a temporary disruption), that result might well be viewed as an equitable adjustment of the cost of capital" (FAS 19, par. 171).

It was believed that "an equitable adjustment" might come about because requiring all firms to use a single, uniform method was better for all users of financial accounting information, including government regulators. The national interest, it asserted, was promoted by its ruling because the free market in the measurement of financial data tends to promote misunderstanding.

> To the extent that furtherance of competition in oil and gas exploration and production and the availability of increased capital resources to finance those efforts are perceived as national economic or policy goals and in the interest of the general public, those goals can best be fostered . . . if all competitors disclose financial data in a marketplace free from the burdens of inconsistency, noncomparability and misunderstanding . . . (FAS 19, par. 172).

From FAS 19 and the above assertions used to support it, a reasonable inference is that required uniformity in all areas of measurement can be justified on the grounds that efficient resource allocation is thereby promoted.

Following the SEC public hearings in 1978 described above, the Commission determined that the two traditional measurements, SE and FC, were both limited and not appropriate because of their failure to provide measurement and disclosure of oil and gas reserves in the primary financial statements. That is, the Commission's position was that the effect of the current value of such reserves on both assets and revenues should be incorporated into the statements. Accordingly, in August 1978, it requested that research begin on a form of current value accounting, and that additions to and changes in the value of proved reserves (reserve recognition accounting) be used on an experimental basis by means of supplemental disclosures for at least three years. It also ruled that both methods which had been used previously (FC and SE) would remain acceptable during that period. Thus, the FASB's decision was overturned.

The FASB then suspended FAS 19 in February 1979 by FAS 25, and, for the second time, the accounting standard setting body in the private sector was required by the SEC to reverse its decision on measurement. The first instance, as described above, was with respect to accounting for the Investment Tax Credit.

F. U.S. DEPARTMENT OF COMMERCE STUDY ON FAS 2

The FASB's expense-only rule for Research and Development (FAS 2), which is the subject of Chapters VII–IX, was approved in October 1974 by a unanimous vote of the seven members. At the end of November 1974, the Board recommended that a broader study of the rule be undertaken. At that time, either because of the Board or independently, the Domestic Business Policy Analysis Staff of the U.S. Department of Commerce (DOC) undertook an interview study. After seven weeks, a report was issued which contained conclusions about the likely economic effects of the uniform expensing rule.

The study, "Impact of FASB's Rule Two Accounting for Research and Development Costs on Small/Developing Stage Firms," indicated that the rule had been criticized by some businessmen, risk investors and government agencies who believed that confusion and misunderstanding by the average investor would follow, and, as a result, R & D investments might be reduced. In addition, the study stated that several executives at the Commerce Department were concerned that changes in methods of measuring profits, either financial or tax, had created problems related to capital formation. Also, it was recognized that there was a need for the government to provide incentives to encourage R & D investment, and therefore any evidence concerning a possible negative impact of FAS 2 on R & D expenditures would be particularly important.

To address this issue, the DOC surveyed small and/or development stage firms, lenders, public accountants, the Internal Revenue Service, and investors (excluding, however, the "average" investor for whom concern had been expressed). With regard to the firms' interviews, the report did not make clear how the sample was selected, no data was reported describing the significance of the R & D outlays for these firms and only 11 managers in total were questioned. Because the purpose of the study was to determine whether adverse consequences would result from requiring firms using the deferral method to switch to the expense method, it would appear that the sample of firms should have come only from those firms which had significant expenditures for R & D and which had been deferring (capitalizing) R & D prior to the change mandated by FAS 2. However, the report indicated that 7 out of the 11 firms interviewed had been expensing prior to No. 2 and therefore were unaffected. The remaining four firms had been deferring.

The survey revealed that three firms planned to reduce their R & D expenditures and four firms stated that they expected an adverse effect on their cost of capital, both types of responses coming as a consequence of Statement 2. The study did not identify whether the three or four firms which claimed negative effects were from the four deferral firms, but such an inference seems reasonable.

The Commerce study's conclusion largely rests on the remaining interviews with 40 lenders and investors (venture capital firms, SBICs, investment banking houses, commercial banks and nonfinancial corporations). Only one out of the 40 stated that its investment policies might change as a consequence of FAS 2; 10 out of the 40 thought that other sophisticated investors might change their investment policies. However, over 40 percent of these sophisticated investors thought that the average investor would limit his investment in those companies affected by the expense-only rule.[2] Additionally, more than 25 percent of the sample believed that some firms might reduce their planned R & D investment as a consequence of the rule.[3]

Unfortunately, the study neither determined the importance of unaffiliated sources of funds (sources other than venture capital firms, SBICs, etc.) to the affected firms nor the attitudes of such sources to the rule change. This exclusion might have been crucial because a study for the National Bureau of Standards showed that unaffiliated individuals provided about 16 percent and "unknown" sources about 25 percent of external sources of funds for small, technology based firms (see Figure IV.1).

Eleven accountants of Big Eight firms were interviewed. It was reported that they were unanimous in their belief that FAS 2 would not lead to a reduction in R & D expenditures and that it would have little, if any, impact on the access to capital of affected firms. This result is surprising in view of public testimony by representatives of the Big Eight during hearings on the rule.[4]

From the above interviews, the DOC reached the conclusion that the impact of the R & D rule would be insignificant. The FASB used the results of the study to support required expensing. The study is cited in FAS 7, *Accounting by Development Stage Enterprises*. There the Board, justifying the elimination of the use of the deferral method for costs of start-up firms, stated that the DOC found that there would be no negative impact from the R & D rule, and the two issues are similar in that the costs of start-up firms, like R & D, are undertaken in the expectation of future benefits.[5]

In sum, the DOC interview study, cited by the FASB to support the adoption of an expense-only rule, concluded that "FASB's Statement Two should not have a significant impact on those firms who have heretofore capitalized R & D." However, the bases for this conclusion appear to be quite weak. Hardly any information was provided about sample selection procedures, and it is not clear that the conclusions drawn from the interview results are warranted. As discussed in Chapter VIII, a more detailed questionnaire study with a larger sample reached a different conclusion.

NOTES

1. The issues related to income smoothing are discussed further in Chapter II.B.

2. In FAS 7, *Accounting and Reporting by Development Stage Enterprises* (par. 49), a concern about the possible adverse effects on the unsophisticated investor also arose. Venture capital enterprises, questioned about their attitudes regarding the elimination of deferred preoperating costs for development stage enterprises, asserted that a mandated switch would have "little effect" ("little" being undefined) on the amount or terms under which venture capital is provided, but that such a mandated switch "might have an impact on the investment and credit decisions of unsophisticated investors."

3. The study also indicated that a typical response was: "A big write-down in reported assets by one of the smalls is bound to hurt them in competing for Government contracts." However, no interviews were conducted with government contracting officers to substantiate that claim.

4. Ernst & Ernst (now Ernst & Whinney), for example, suggested that it believed that a negative impact would follow.

[A]n arbitrary standard calling for the immediate expensing of all research and development expenditures might actually discourage research and development. . . . Unfortunately, there is no means by which to measure or assess the ultimate cost to our economy . . . but the impact will be real all the same. . . . The FASB . . . has opted for uniformity at the expense of equity and more informative reporting. . . . Faced with a decision between accepting heavy immediate charges against net income in order to support research directed at possibly distant future revenues, or reducing current research and development efforts to costs that current income can "afford," some managements may see no alternatives except to penalize the future in order to protect current income (Ernst & Ernst, 1974).

5. It should be noted that the Board believed that the DOC study was confined to R & D outlays of development stage firms (FAS 7, par. 50). However, the study focused "on developing stage companies as defined by the FASB and small operating companies" (DOC, 1975). The six responses to a letter sent by the authors to the 11 companies interviewed by the DOC showed that three did not file as developing stage companies with the SEC and two were private companies.

Chapter VII

Issues Related to R & D Reporting

In December 1973 the Financial Accounting Standards Board released a Discussion Memorandum on alternative accounting and reporting practices for R & D costs. This was followed by a public hearing in March 1974, the issuance of an Exposure Draft (ED) in June 1974, the receipt of letters evaluating the ED and, finally, in October 1974 the publication of FAS 2, *Accounting for Research and Development Costs,* effective for annual reports issued after January 1, 1975. In October 1975 the Securities and Exchange Commission accepted FAS 2 in ASR 178 which applied to all financial statements filed with the SEC. Both regulations required that all research and development (R & D) costs be charged to expense when incurred.[1]

Discussion in this chapter focuses on several issues related to the above requirement. Similarities and differences between the events surrounding the adoption of these rules and events surrounding the consideration of other rules are explored. Finally, this chapter contains a review of arguments made in support of the R & D rule and evidence of the contribution to the innovation process by affected firms.

A. HYPOTHESIZED EFFECTS OF FAS 2

There has been little concern about the possible consequences of mandated changes in measurement rules which are used in external financial reporting. In fact, as discussed in detail in Chapter IV, except for the discussion of the alleged, but unsupported, consequences of the proposal to mandate the use of the deferral method for reporting the investment tax credit in the 1960s, there was not much serious debate about the economic effects of involuntary changes in measurement rules prior to the public hearings held in 1978 by the SEC. The particular subject of those hearings was the appropriate accounting method for reporting exploration and development costs in the oil and gas industry, but a significant underlying question was whether mandating a uniform reporting rule could produce adverse economic effects.

Most studies of changes in measurement rules, either voluntary or involuntary, have concentrated on security price effects, examining possible changes in systematic risk or abnormal return residuals. Little research, however, has been performed to assess the internal firm effects on investment activity of changes in measurement rules. Although, as mentioned above, suggestions were made about the direct effects of the investment tax credit, no empirical data became available because the expressed fears of adverse consequences resulted in a suspension of that rule. Thus, in 1962 when the Accounting Principles Board (now the FASB) mandated the deferral method of accounting for the investment tax credit, the SEC rejected the rule because, among other reasons, it was believed that investment would be greater if companies were allowed freedom in choosing measurement methods. Because the Accounting Principles Board subseqently revoked its own rule, there was no opportunity to test that belief.

The measurement issue which generated controversy in the oil and gas industry in 1978 was straightforward: Whether explorations and drilling costs for unsuccessful oil and gas wells should be deferred or expensed in order to achieve a single, uniform reporting system. The FASB in Statement 19 required all companies to. expense those outlays ("successful efforts"), but the SEC, having oversight responsibility for financial reporting given to it by Congress, was required to conduct hearings to determine whether the rule was anticompetitive.[2,3]

Testimony at the oil and gas hearings, as noted in Chapter VI, raised doubts about the neutrality of the mandated rule on companies that would be affected. Although several respondents who supported the likelihood of anti-competitive effects at those hearings explained the FASB's conclusion as an effort to maintain consistency with the Board's earlier decision requiring the immediate write-off of R & D outlays, no one suggested that, for reasons similar to oil and gas, FAS 2 might also have anticompetitive effects (FTC, 1978). The reason may be attributed to the belief that most companies were expensing R & D prior to the rule, and the fact that the opposition, coming mainly from small firms dispersed over a number of industries, was not vocal and resulted in little, if any, organized lobbying effort.

Statements similar to those cited in Chapter VI from the oil and gas hearings were made by small company representatives during the FASB hearings on the R & D measurement issue. In addition, both prior to the adoption of the R & D rule and later when there was a re-examination of FASB Statements 1–12, several large CPA firms stated that the rule might be harmful if it encouraged companies to reduce their R & D outlays. Ernst & Ernst, for example, in a brief on the FASB Exposure Draft asserted that ". . . immediate expensing of all research and development expenditures by all companies in all conditions might actually discourage research and development." It added that ". . . there is no means by which to measure or assess the ultimate cost to our economy in terms of economic progress if the proposed standard is made effective" (FASB, 1974, p. 448).

Furthermore, Coopers & Lybrand, responding to a request for re-examination of the Statements, stated in August 1978, three full years after Rule 2 became effective, that: ". . . the immediate expense recognition method required by FASB Statement No. 2 . . . may influence research and development spending decisions. If the immediate earnings impact becomes an important factor in making these expenditure decisions, there may be an adverse long-term economic impact on these companies" (Coopers & Lybrand, 1978).

It was not possible to test the assertions of a reduction in exploration activity by small oil and gas producers because the SEC refused to accept FAS 19 and it was subsequently suspended (FAS 25, 1979). Thus, unlike the R & D rule, both the proposal to mandate the deferral method to report the tax savings of the investment credit and the proposal to mandate a single method (expensing) to report exploration and development costs were never enacted because of claimed economic consequences. Consequently, no tests could be performed on the actual effects of these proposed measurement rules on firm behavior. The adoption of No. 2, however, permitted a "laboratory experiment" to test whether this rule impacted the R & D investment decisions of affected firms. Aside from the importance of attempting to determine the answer to the general question of the economic impact of a mandated rule change, information with respect to the specific effects of the R & D rule is important because of the crucial role which company-sponsored R & D expenditures have in economic growth and productivity.

Evidence, tests and conclusions related to the R & D issue are presented in Chapters VIII and IX. Strong doubts are expressed there about the neutrality of the expense-only rule for R & D. The remainder of this chapter provides additional background material.

B. R & D REPORTING IN OTHER COUNTRIES

The adoption of FAS 2 by the FASB and the SEC made the United States the only country that requires the expensing of all R & D outlays. After it was adopted, the accounting bodies of other countries considered the various methods of measuring R & D and came to the conclusion that the expense-only rule was too rigid and that development projects satisfying certain criteria should be or may be deferred. These countries included Canada, the U.K., Australia, France and the European Economic Community. In July 1978, the International Accounting Standards Committee, consisting of the above countries plus Japan, Mexico and the U.S., ruled that deferral should be permitted when stated criteria are met. Presently, Canada and Australia *require* deferral under the same stated criteria.[4]

C. SUPPORT FOR FAS 2

The FASB's support of the expense-only rule was based on a number of arguments. It was contended that expensing better reflects the uncertain nature of risk,[5] that there was no empirical evidence demonstrating a significant correlation between R & D outlays and future sales, profits or share of industry sales,[6] and that security analysts, professional investors and bankers who either submitted their views at the public hearing or were interviewed by the Board suggested that capitalization was not useful (FAS 2, pars. 41, 50, 54).[7]

Another argument propounded was that under selective capitalization it is difficult to define precise criteria and, therefore, the requirement to expense would prevent abuse by management which otherwise would occur because of a "loose" definition. "Abuses" in R & D accounting were thought to be reflected in the past by a few large companies writing off significant amounts of capitalized R & D.[8]

Related to this is the fact that the simplicity of the expensing method reduces auditors' risk of liability. It has been suggested that the expense-only rule was generally supported by the public accounting profession because it removed the greater judgment required for deferral and subsequent amortization, and, therefore, possible legal liability. The SEC has been sensitive to the possibility that the Board's development of disclosure rules may be influenced by its concern with the legal liability of auditors. However, it is not apparent that it considered whether this concern applies equally to measurement rules for financial reporting. With respect to disclosure, for example, Harold Williams, Chairman of the Securities and Exchange Commission, commented:

> ... the argument most frequently voiced against disclosure of more relevant data is that it would sacrifice the existing objectively verifiable basis for primary financial statements. This notion of recognizing only so-called "hard" data is deeply ingrained in both accountants and accounting literature The very real risks of monetary liability which have become a daily fact of life in the auditing profession make this attitude quite understandable. Yet, dogmatic adherence to this concept prevents effective consideration and response to the resulting disclosure inadequacies in a changing economic climate (1979).

D. R & D REPORTING METHOD AND FIRM SIZE

A large number of respondents to the Exposure Draft on R & D which preceded Statement 2, and many of those who appeared at the hearings to discuss this draft, emphasized that expensing was reasonable because most companies were already using that method, particularly the larger companies.[9,10] As an article (*Barrons*, 1974, p. 3) observed shortly after the rule was passed: "the FASB acknowledges that it had a relatively easy time with its decision, since fewer than 20 percent of the publicly owned corporations defer R & D, and most were small, with little clout."

Opposition to expensing voiced at the hearings came primarily from academics, spokesmen for small companies, and the venture capital industry. Two typical responses opposing expensing were: (1) a small company president—"Innovators are a diverse, scattered, small company type of group. They will not mobilize as a group for any purpose much less to oppose accounting or legal rule changes however consequential . . ."; (2) a spokesman for the National Venture Capital Association, an important supplier of funds for start-up and small, growing companies—"Although the effect of the Exposure Draft would be to greatly simplify the auditor's job . . . it would also have the undesirable effect of . . . perhaps causing established companies to forego important new development projects. . . ." (FASB, 1974, pp. 133, 584).[11]

Existing evidence supports the assertion that the deferral method was much more widely used among smaller companies. After selecting industries with high concentrations of R & D, San Miguel (1975, p. II–83) selected 173 firms having an identifiable policy for R & D outlays in 1972. An analysis by size of company showed that about 90 percent of companies with sales over $1 billion had an expense-only policy, whereas almost 50 percent of the companies with less than $10 million of sales used this method (see Table VII.1).

Other surveys (Orton and Bradish, 1969; Gellein and Newman, 1973) confirm this distribution. The Gellein and Newman study for the AICPA showed that of 245 companies studied, about 96 percent wrote-off R & D costs in the period during which they were incurred, but that the smaller companies ("more recently developed companies") showed a greater tendency toward deferral. The questionnaire study by Orton and Bradish indicated overwhelming support for expensing, but again this support came from large companies. Finally, a perusal of the recommendations made by corporate representatives to both the Discussion Memorandum and the Exposure

Table VII.1. R & D Accounting Policy Disclosed, 173 Firms by 1972 Sales Volume

| Sales Volume | Accounting Policy | | | | | | Total Disclosures | |
| | Expense | | Capitalize | | Combination | | | |
	#	%	#	%	#	%	#	%
$1 Billion Plus	31	89%	1	3%	3	8%	35	20%
$500–999 Million	21	91			2	9	23	13
$250–499 Million	19	76	1	4	5	20	25	15
$100–249 Million	29	88			4	12	33	19
$ 10– 99 Million	33	70	6	13	8	17	47	27
Less than $10 Million	5	50	3	30	2	20	10	6
	138%	80%	11	6%	24	14%	173	100%

Source: San Miguel, J., p. II–83.

Draft also suggests that the expense advocates were almost entirely from large companies.

E. INNOVATION AND SMALL BUSINESS

An important reason for examining the specific impact of FAS 2 relates to the fact that many of the firms which had been deferring R & D prior to the rule were small, high-technology firms. Because these firms make a disproportionately large contribution to the innovation process, even small effects on their R & D may have a significant effect on innovation.[12]

Both the real growth of privately funded R & D outlay and its quality, as manifested in new technology and innovation, have recently come under close scrutiny in the United States because of a concern with the retardation of the growth in productivity. This concern has generally been associated with the rate of growth of R & D for all industry, but a few studies have tended to focus on small business, particularly high-technology firms.

Many studies have shown that small companies have a comparative advantage over large firms in the innovation process. A recent study by the National Science Foundation concluded that, in the 1953–1973 period, firms with less than 1,000 employees were responsible for half of the "most significant new industrial products and processes" (Joint Hearings, 1978, p. 432). Firms with 100 or less employees produced 24 percent of such innovations. Although such firms accounted for only three percent of the total dollar value of R & D, they produced 24 times more major innovations per research dollar expended as did large firms (Joint Hearings, 1978).

Empirical research on the question of size of the firm and the productivity of R & D seems to indicate that, while large firms are better able to exploit the results of R & D, small firms tend to develop R & D innovations more efficiently. Mansfield, et al. (1971) has estimated that, for the 1935-1949 period, the ratio of the number of innovations to sales for the drug industry reached a maximum at a sales level of $10 million. In the 1950-1962 period, the maximum value of this ratio was at a sales level of $20 million which, at that time, corresponded to the twelfth largest firm in the industry.

Mansfield's study on R & D outlays in the chemical industry shows decreasing returns to scale after a modest size, and Schmookler's study on patents found that larger firms are less efficient in patent development (a gauge of innovative activity) than smaller firms (Kamien and Schwartz, 1975, pp. 9-10). Jewkes, et al. (1969) showed that over half of the 61 important inventions and innovations of the twentieth century came from the activities of independent inventors and small firms. Peck (1962) studied 149 inventions in the processing and finishing of aluminum and concluded that major producers accounted for only one of seven important inventions. Enos evaluated seven major inventions for the refining and cracking of petroleum and concluded that none of them came from large companies (Joint Hearings, 1978, p. 527). From the studies cited above, it is apparent that the R & D activities of small firms are particularly important to the innovation process in this country.

F. SUMMARY

The expense-only rule for research and development is unique to the U.S. among industrialized countries. Effective for annual reports appearing after January 1, 1975, the rule affected mainly small high-technology companies, a large percentage of which had previously used the deferral method. Predictably, objections to the rule during public hearings came from representatives of these small firms. Because these firms have an important role in the innovation process, any regulation which could have negatively affected them needs to be more thoroughly examined.

NOTES

1. The regulations also more precisely defined R & D, making it closer to the definition used by the National Science Foundation. One remaining difference, however, was that the NSF definition did not include some social science activities in service-type industries (FASB, 1974, par. 28). Later, evidence is provided which shows that the effect of the definitional change alone, apart from real changes, was immaterial. (See response to question on the change in R & D classification in Appendix VIII.B.)

2. The requirement resulted from a June 4, 1975 Amendment to the SEC 1934 Act, 15 USC, par. 78 w(a)(2), discussed in Chapter III.C.

3. This rule and evidence of its effects are detailed in Chapter VI. Discussion here is limited to a comparison with Statement 2.

4. The position of the U.S. relative to other countries has been well stated: "To all [U.S.] bodies studying the issue, however, it eventually became clear that, although they could possibly specify criteria that, if met, *permitted* capitalization, they could not specify criteria that, if met, would effectively *require* capitalization in similar circumstances," and "A selective capitalization standard was not likely to . . . relieve the discomfort of auditors forced to accept either expensing or capitalization under essentially identical circumstances" (Sprouse, 1979, p. 58).

5. The arguments with respect to whether "true" risk and income is derived from a capitalization or expensing policy are not reviewed here. It may be noted, however, that the question has still not been resolved either by academicians (Bierman and Dukes, 1975) or practitioners.

6. The Board, itself, presented no empirical research on the economics of R & D but cited three accounting studies. In a public letter to the Board, the author of one of these studies, however, denied the validity of the Board's conclusion of no correlation from his study.

7. One exception to the R & D rule which was made by the Board was for government regulated enterprises. They were allowed to defer although they had to disclose their amortization policy and the amounts capitalized. No evidence was provided, however, that for these organizations future benefits of R & D are more certain or that the aforementioned correlation is significant.

8. Large write-offs were publicized for General Dynamics, Lockheed, McDonnell Douglas Aircraft, and Ampex.

9. "[Expensing] is supremely practical, especially in view of a comprehensive Elmo Roper and Associates survey of existing practice showing that . . . only a few respondents deferred R & D costs" (Sprouse, 1979, p. 58).

10. Among the several exceptions were the Sperry Rand Corporation, the president of which argued that deferral is needed when the company is small. ". . . I can say quite candidly that Univac would not be here today if we had not had the advantage of the old rule for so many years" (*Business Week,* July 3, 1978, p. 52).

11. Interestingly, in a related area, the Louisiana Public Service Commission objected to South Central Bell expensing R & D. "Reflection on the nature of research and development effort will show that it is an improper rate making treatment to currently expense the cost associated with research and development. By definition, research and development effort is undertaken to find new or improved processes or products and new facts which will enhance the future welfare of South Central Bell" (Louisiana Public Service Commission, 1976).

12. In an interview survey conducted five years after FAS 2 (Yankelovich, Skelly and White, Inc., 1980), among 101 R & D and senior operating executives of companies in 20 industries having significant outlays of R & D, concern was expressed about the negative impact of FAS 2 on innovation.

Chapter VIII

Management Attitudes Toward the R & D Rule

The only prior research on the cost/benefit impact of FAS 2 was not undertaken until after the Board had reached its decision in October 1974. As explained in Chapter VI.F, that research, which primarily consisted of a survey of institutional investors, was performed neither by the Board nor by the SEC but by the Department of Commerce (DOC) which was concerned about the recent decline in R & D outlays and the need to assist innovation (U.S. Department of Commerce, 1975, p. 2).

The DOC study concluded that FAS 2 would not have a significant impact on those firms which had used the capitalization (deferral) method. This conclusion was cited by the Board in a later Statement to support the position that mandated uniformity would not cause economic harm (FAS 7, par. 50). However, as noted in Chapter VI.F, many aspects of the DOC study raise questions; the sampling method is not discussed, and the conclusion is neither strong nor based upon any statistical tests.

Because of the limited scope and the deficiencies of the DOC survey and because at the hearings prior to the issuance of FAS 2 it was stated repeatedly that small businesses would not make an effort to express their opinions even though the measurement issue would significantly affect them, the authors developed a questionnaire to survey managers of small companies concerning their beliefs and attitudes toward the R & D rule. Specifically, the purpose of the questionnaire was to provide additional background material on the R & D issue, to aid in the identification of possible firm reactions to FAS 2, and to contradict or support the results of statistical tests performed on actual changes in R & D behavior reported in the next chapter.

A. METHODOLOGY AND RESULTS

The survey was conducted during the Spring of 1979. Questionnaires were sent to the chief financial officers of 380 firms. Of these, 168 companies had deferred and 212 had expensed R & D outlays prior to Statement 2. The 168 deferral firms were compiled from several editions of the *Disclosure Journal*, subject to the condition that they be listed in *Moody's OTC Manual* (1978). The expense firms were selected from the OTC Compustat Listing, provided that their R & D expenditures were at least one percent of sales and 5 percent of net income after tax. The total sample was distributed among 19 two digit SIC industries with about 22 percent from machinery (other than electrical), and 23 percent from electrical and electronic machinery, equipment, and supplies. Table VIII.1 contains a detailed breakdown of responding firms by industry and by R & D reporting method prior to No. 2. Overall, replies to the questionnaire were received from 131 companies, a response rate of 34 percent.

The questionnaire instrument is presented in Appendix VIII.A. Requested was information concerning the firm's level of R & D expenditures (questions 5, 11, 12); the reporting method prior to Statement 2 (question 1); definitional changes in the types of outlays classified as R & D (question 2); variability of research and development (question 4); access to capital markets (questions 9, 10); risk and length of life of R & D projects (questions 3, 6); and opinions as to the appropriateness of the deferral method (questions 8, 13, 14, 15, 16, and 17).

The responses of companies are reported and analyzed in two ways in Appendix VIII.B. First the responses of companies that had been deferring R & D prior to the expense-only rule were compared to the responses of those that had been expensing (Appendix VIII.B, Tables 1–3). Secondly, the responses were analyzed by firm size (Appendix VIII.B, Tables 4–6).

Examining first the differences between deferral and expense firms, the results indicate that there are significant differences (at the .05 level) in the responses of key managers of

Table VIII.1. Responding Firms by Industry and Reporting Method

(1) Industry	(2) Two-Digit SIC Code	(3) Number-Deferred	(4) Number-Expensed	(5) Total**	(6) % Total Sample
Metal Mining	10	0		1*	.0078
Oil and Gas Extraction	13		1	1	.0078
Building Construction	15	1		1*	.0078
Food and Kindred Products	20		1	2	.0155
Printing, Publishing, and Allied Industries	27	2	0	2	.0155
Chemicals and Allied Products	28	2	8	10	.0775
Rubber and Miscellaneous Plastic Products	30	0	1	1	.0078
Primary Metal Industries	33	1	0	1	.0078
Fabricated Metal Products, Except Machinery and Transportation Equipment	34	2	7	9	.0698
Machinery, except Electrical	35	8	20	29*	.2248
Electrical and Electronic Machinery, Equipment, and Supplies	36	6	22	30*	.2326
Transportation Equipment	37	2	1	3	.0233
Measuring, Analyzing, and Controlling Instruments	38	7	14	21	.1628
Electric, Gas, and Sanitary Services	49	1	0	1	.0078
Wholesale Trade-Nondurable Goods	51	0	1	1	.0078
Holding and Other Investment Officer	67	1	0	1	.0078
Business services	73	8	5	13	.1008
Health Services	80	0	1	1	.0078
Miscellaneous Services	89	0	1	1	.0078

Notes: *Total of columns (3) and (4) may not equal column (5) due to inability to identify method of reporting for some companies.
**Based on 129 companies of the sample with known standard industrial codes.

these firms regarding: (1) the change in emphasis on R & D in the respondent's firm since FAS 2 (greater decline in emphasis by deferral firms); (2) the difficulty created in the evaluation of the performance of small firms by unsophisticated investors (greater perceived difficulty on the part of the deferral firms); (3) the appropriateness of the deferral method for young firms (deferral firms replying more often that it is appropriate); (4) the need for small firms to choose between expensing and capitalizing R & D for financial statement purposes (deferral firms responding more often that the need exists); and (5) the change in the method of tax reporting (deferral firms changing methods more often).

Question No. 5 was one of the few questions which was related specifically to the behavior of the respondent firm itself. As indicated above, there was a significant difference between the deferral and the expense respondents with respect to the change in emphasis placed on R & D since the adoption of No. 2. The responses to this question, indicating that there were greater reductions in emphasis placed on R & D by firms previously deferring relative to those which had been expensing, are consistent with the empirical findings discussed in Chapter IX.

The responses of the two sets of firms to the question, "Do you think R & D outlays for some small companies would be greater if the deferral option were still available?"—although not significantly different—indicate that 65.8 percent of the deferral companies and 54.3 percent of the expense companies believed that this is or might be true. Comments provided by managers responding affirmatively to this question suggest that the lower reported earnings which result from the expensing method limit R & D outlays because of financing difficulties and the dividend obligations of the firms.

There also was no statistical difference in the responses of the two groups to the question, "Do you believe that Statement No. 2 makes it more difficult and/or more expensive for some small firms to raise capital?" What is particularly surprising is that 65 percent of the deferral group and 50 percent of the expense group answered either "yes" or "possibly." Again, the respondents' comments on this question emphasized that research and development outlays had to be restrained because otherwise profit would be adversely affected.

Of particular importance is the response to question 15b. Almost 93 percent of the deferral firms expected that the unsophisticated investor had at least some difficulty evaluating the profit performance of small companies because of FAS 2. The percent of expensing firms which expressed this belief also was extremely high, 75.3 percent. As indicated in Chapter VII, the unsophisticated investor is an important source of equity funds for small, high technology firms and therefore his investment behavior is particularly critical to such companies. The Department of Commerce study recognized the importance of this source of funds but made no further analysis because it claimed that information about it was unavailable.

In sum, the above results suggest that a significant number of the officers surveyed believe that the expense-only rule had negative effects. This is true for both deferral and expensing firms although the belief is more widespread among deferral firms, as expected.

Tables 4, 5 and 6 of Appendix VIII.B examine responses to the questionnaire by firm size as measured by sales revenue. The greatest significant differences between the responses of small and large firms relate to the issue of difficulty in the evaluation of the performance of small firms, changes in the yearly variability of R & D, and changes in the method of tax reporting for R & D. Firms with sales less than $10 million responded significantly more often than larger firms that the deferral method is appropriate, that both methods should be available, that mandating the expense method will cause difficulty in assessing a firm's performance, and that the variability of R & D expenditure would increase.

To some questions there was surprisingly strong agreement among all firms. In response to the question, "Do you believe that some small firms reduced planned R & D expenditures as a consequence of FASB No. 2," 66.7 percent of firms with sales less than $10 million and 58.9 percent of firms with sales greater than $10 million answered affirmatively or possibly. There also was strong agreement that R & D outlays would possibly be greater if the deferral option were still available

(68.2 percent of smaller firms; 52.2 percent of larger firms), and there was concern among all firms that the unsophisticated investor will have at least some difficulty in evaluating the performance of the small firm (88.1 percent of the smaller firms and 77.6 percent of the larger firms responded so).

Also noteworthy were the responses of the two groups regarding the perceived difficulty that suppliers and government agencies would have in evaluating an affected firm's performance—once again, a high percentage of respondents from both groups agreed that those two sources of funds, both critical to the growth of small firms, will encounter at least some difficulty in evaluating performance.

Finally, it should be noted that (1) the majority of all companies responded that the expense-only rule will make it more difficult and/or more expensive to raise capital; (2) over 60 percent of the firms with less than $10 million in sales expressed the belief that even the sophisticated investor will be affected by No. 2; and (3) Tables 1 and 4 of Appendix VIII.B indicate that over 73 percent of both small firms and deferral firms believed that the deferral method is an appropriate one for small firms.

B. CONCLUSIONS

Clearly, the survey results discussed in this chapter lead to conclusions that are sharply different from the previously discussed Department of Commerce study upon which the FASB relied. Many of the chief financial officers of small, high-technology firms, analyzed either by measurement method or by firm size, perceived that the expense-only rule for R & D negatively affected the ability of some firms to raise capital and, ultimately, their R & D expenditures.

Managements' perceptions, in themselves, are crucial because of the effect that they have on investment decisions. If, as suggested by the questionnaire results, managers believed that small firms were placed at a disadvantage with respect to their ability to raise funds, this alone may have led to a reduction in R & D. The next chapter considers whether such a reduction occurred.

APPENDIX VIII.A

Research & Development Questionnaire

1. For *EXTERNAL* reporting purposes (*Annual Report* and S. E. C. 10-K), did your company expense or defer R&D outlays prior to January 1, 1975 (or prior to the date when the company was affected by "Statement of Financial Accounting Standards No. 2," *Accounting for Research and Development Costs*)?

   Expense ......□   Defer ....□   Both expense and defer ....□

2. Were there any significant definitional changes in the types of outlays classified as R&D for *EXTERNAL* reporting purposes as a result of the No. 2 Standard (affecting more than 5% of R&D)?

   Yes ....□   No.................□   Don't know ....□

   Additional Comment: (IF ANSWER WAS "YES," PLEASE DESCRIBE BRIEFLY)

   _____

   _____

3. Since January 1, 1975, has there been any change in the median length of time for completion of R&D proposals, i.e., from the time of the conception of an idea to the beginning of commercialization?

   No change .□   Probably decreased ....□   Probably increased .....□   Unknown ....□

   Additional Comment:

   _____

   _____

4. Since January 1, 1975, has the pattern of R&D in your company changed relative to an equal period prior to 1975 in any of the ways indicated below?

   There has been greater variation in year-to-year R&D expenditures ....□

   There has been greater stability in year-to-year R&D expenditures ....□

   There has been no significant change in the pattern of zear-to-year R&D expenditures ....□

   Don't know ....□

Additional Comment:

_____

_____

_____

5. Since January 1, 1975, has the emphasis placed on R&D within your firm changed (relative to change in the size of your company) in any of the ways indicated below?

        There has been a relative increase in emphasis on R&D ......□
        There has been a relative decrease in emphasis on R&D ......□
        No significant change ....□
        Don't know ....□

Additional Comment:

_____

_____

6. Since January 1, 1975, has the focus of R&D efforts in your company shifted in any of the ways indicated below? *(CHECK AS MANY AS ARE RELEVANT)*

More focus today on R&D projects with nearer term benefits ....□   More focus today on less risky R&D projects ....□

More focus today on R&D projects with longer term benefits ....□   None of the above ....□

More focus today on more risky R&D projects ....□   Don't know ....□

Additional Comment:

_____

_____

7. Prior to January 1, 1975, did your company expense or defer R&D outlays for *TAX* purposes?

                             Both expense
Expense ..□   Defer ....□   and defer ....□   Don't know ...□

8. After January 1, 1975, did your company change its tax reporting for R&D outlays?

Change ....□   No change ....□   Don't know ....□

Additional Comment (IF ANSWER WAS "CHANGE," PLEASE BRIEFLY DESCRIBE WHY)

_____

_____

9. Do you believe that potential investors are less inclined to invest in developing-stage firms (5 to 10 years old) or start-up firms (less than 5 years old) because of the impact of the No. 2 Standard on those firms' financial statements?

Yes ..... □   Possibly ...... □   No .... □   No opinion .... □
Additional Comment:

_____

_____

10. Do you believe that the No. 2 Standard makes it more difficult and/or more expensive for some small firms to raise capital?
Yes ..... □   Possibly ...... □   No .... □   No opinion ... □
Additional Comment: (IF ANSWER WAS "YES" OR POSSIBLY," PLEASE BRIEFLY DESCRIBE WHY)

_____

_____

11. Do you think R&D outlays for some small companies would be greater if the deferral option were still available?
Yes ..... □   Possibly ...... □   No .... □   No opinion ... □
Additional Comment: (IF ANSWER WAS "YES" OR "POSSIBLY," PLEASE BRIEFLY DESCRIBE WHY)

_____

_____

12. Do you believe that some small firms reduced *PLANNED* R&D expenditures as a consequence of the No. 2 Standard?
Yes ..... □   Possibly ...... □   No .... □   No opinion ... □

13. Does your company use the deferral method for the *INTERNAL* evaluation of divisions and/or projects?
Never .... □   Rarely .... □   Often .... □   Always .... □

14. Do you think it is appropriate to defer R&D connected with:

	Always Appropriate	Sometimes Appropriate	Never Appropriate	No Opinion
a. Small firms in general	□	□	□	□
b. Developing-stage firms ,..........	□	□	□	□
c. New product division of small firms	□	□	□	□
d. Expanding use of existing product of small firms ...	□	□	□	□

Additional Comment:

_____

_____

15. Does the expensing of R&D expenditures as incurred create difficulty in evaluating the profit performance of small companies?

	Considerable Difficulty	Some Difficulty	No Difficulty	No Opinion
a. By the sophisticated investor	☐	☐	☐	☐
b. By the unsophisticated investor	☐	☐	☐	☐
c. By suppliers	☐	☐	☐	☐
d. By government agencies	☐	☐	☐	☐

Additional Comment:

_____

_____

_____

16. Do you believe that small firms should be able to choose between expensing and capitalizing R&D for financial reporting purposes?

Yes, all firms ..☐   Yes, some firms ...☐   No ....☐   No opinion ...☐

Additional Comment:

_____

_____

_____

17. What was you company's position on accounting Standard No. 2?

Supported ....☐   Did not support ......☐   Indifferent ...☐   Don't know ...☐

Additional Comment:

_____

_____

_____

_____

_____

_____

_____

THANK YOU FOR YOUR ASSISTANCE. PLEASE MAIL BACK YOUR COMPLETED QUESTIONNAIRE IN THE ENCLOSED ENVELOPE.

Appendix B. Table 1. Appropriateness of Deferral Method

Questions 14, 15 and 16	Deferral Firm Responses			Expense Firm Responses			Tests for Differences	
	Always	*Sometimes*	*Never*	*Always*	*Sometimes*	*Never*	*df*	χ^2
Appropriateness of deferral method for:								
Small firms in general	9.8%	63.4%	26.8%	5.7%	45.7%	48.6%	2	5.151 (.0761)
Developing-stage Firms	24.4	48.8	26.8	5.6	50.7	43.7	2	9.298 (.0096)
New Product Division	12.5	57.5	30.0	8.5	45.1	46.5	2	2.935 (.2305)
Existing Products/Small firm	5.1	38.5	56.4	4.4	27.9	67.6	2	1.383 (.5008)
Difficulty Created in Evaluation of Performance of Small Firms by:	*Considerable*	*Some*	*None*	*Considerable*	*Some*	*None*		
Sophisticated Investor	7.3%	41.5%	51.2%	2.6%	31.6%	65.8%	2	3.042 (.2185)
Unsophisticated Investor	65.0	27.5	7.5	36.2	39.1	24.6	2	9.514 (.0086)
Suppliers	33.3	44.4	22.2	19.1	50.0	30.9	2	2.763 (.2512)
Government Agencies	32.3	38.7	29.0	19.4	33.9	46.8	2	3.183 (.2036)
Choice of Deferral of Expensing Should be Available to Small Firms:	*Yes, All*	*Yes, Some*	*No*	*Yes, All*	*Yes, Some*	*No*		
	35.9%	25.6%	38.5%	26.2%	10.0%	63.7%	2	8.093 (.0175)

Appendix B. Table 2. Effect on Level of Expenditures and Cost of Capital

Questions 11, 12, 5, 10 and 9	Deferral Firm Responses			Expense Firm Responses			Tests for Difference	
	Yes	*Possibly*	*No*	*Yes*	*Possibly*	*No*	*df*	χ^2
Greater R & D Outlays if Deferral Option Still Available	42.1%	23.7%	34.2%	18.6%	35.7%	45.7%	2	6.995 (.0303)
Reduction in *Planned* R & D Expenditures as a Consequence of FASB No. 2	28.9	42.1	28.9	20.0	36.7	43.3	2	2.246 (.3252)
Change in Emphasis on R & D in Respondent's Firm	*Increase* 25.6%	*Decrease* 28.2%	*No Change* 46.2%	*Increase* 41.5%	*Decrease* 11.0%	*No Change* 47.6%	2	6.577 (.0373)
More Difficult and/or More Expensive to Raise Capital	*Yes* 35.0%	*Possibly* 30.0%	*No* 35.0%	*Yes* 18.3%	*Possibly* 31.7%	*No* 50.0%	2	3.915 (.1412)
Reduction in Investment in Developing Stage Firms	30.6	16.7	52.8	12.7	23.6	63.6	2	4.435 (.1089)

Appendix B. Table 3.   Other Potential Effects

Questions 6, 4, 3, 2 and 8	Deferral Firm Responses			Expense Firm Responses			Tests for Differences	
							df	χ^2
Change in Closeness of Benefits from R & D Projects	*Nearer* 50.0%	*Longer* 17.6%	*Neither* 32.4%	*Nearer* 35.3%	*Longer* 27.9%	*Neither* 36.8%	2	2.325 (.3128)
Change in Risk of R & D Projects	*More* 0.0	*Less* 54.2	*Neither* 45.8	*More* 7.3	*Less* 31.7	*Neither* 61.0	2	4.292 (.1170)
Change in Yearly Variability of R & D	*More Variable* 40.5	*More Stable* 13.5	*No Change* 45.9	*More Variable* 21.7	*More Stable* 9.6	*No Change* 68.7	2	5.807 (.548)
Change in R & D Proposal Completion Time	*No Change* 75.0	*Probably Decreased* 6.3	*Probably Increased* 18.8	*No Change* 58.0	*Probably Decreased* 7.2	*Probably Increased* 34.8	2	2.924 (.2318)
Change of Classification of R & D	*Yes* 7.3	*No* 92.7		*Yes* 3.7	*No* 96.3		2	.8373 (.6682)
Change in Method of Tax Reporting for R & D	*Change* 28.2	*No Change* 71.8		*Change* 2.4	*No Change* 97.6		1	16.159 (.0001)

Appendix B. Table 4. Appropriateness of Deferral Method

Questions 14, 15 and 16	Responses: Firms with < $10mm Sales			Responses: Firms with > $10mm Sales			Tests for Differences	
Appropriateness of Deferral Method for:	*Always*	*Sometimes*	*Never*	*Always*	*Sometimes*	*Never*	*df*	χ^2
Small Firms in General	8.9%	64.4%	26.7%	6.1%	43.9%	50.0%	2	6.043 (.0487)
Developing-stage Firms	20.0	55.6	24.4	7.5	46.3	46.3	2	7.269 (.0264)
New Product Division/Small Firm	13.6	63.6	22.7	7.5	40.3	52.2	2	9.646 (.0080)
Existing Products/Small Firm	7.1	42.9	50.0	3.1	24.6	72.3	2	5.572 (.0617)
Difficulty Created in Evaluation of Performance of Small Firms by:	*Considerable*	*Some*	*None*	*Considerable*	*Some*	*None*		
Sophisticated Investor	6.7%	55.6%	37.8%	2.8%	22.2%	75.0%		16.083 (.0003)
Unsophisticated Investor	59.5	28.6	11.9	38.8	38.8	22.4	2	4.690 (.0958)
Suppliers	39.0	46.3	14.6	14.3	49.2	36.5	2	10.627 (.0049)
Government Agencies	27.0	48.6	24.3	21.4	26.8	51.8	2	7.408 (.0246)
Choice of Deferral of Expensing Should be Available to Small Firms	*Yes, All*	*Yes, Some*	*No*	*Yes, All*	*Yes, Some*	*No*		
	40.0%	22.2%	37.8%	23.0%	10.8%	66.2%	2	9.248 (.0098)

Appendix B. Table 5. Effect on Level of Expenditures and Cost of Capital

Questions 11, 12, 5, 10 and 9	Responses: Firms with < $10mm Sales			Responses: Firms with > $10mm Sales			Tests for difference	
	Yes	*Possibly*	*No*	*Yes*	*Possibly*	*No*	*df*	χ^2
Greater R & D Outlays if Deferral Option Still Available	34.1%	34.1%	31.7%	22.4%	29.9%	47.8%	2	3.032 (.2196)
Reduction in *Planned* R & D Expenditures as a Consequence of FASB No. 2	28.6	38.1	33.3	19.6	39.3	41.1	2	1.205 (.5475)
	Increase	*Decrease*	*No Change*	*Increase*	*Decrease*	*No Change*		
Change in Emphasis on R & D in Respondent's Firm	28.9%	24.4%	46.7%	40.8%	11.8%	47.7%	2	3.820 (.1481)
	Yes	*Possibly*	*No*	*Yes*	*Possibly*	*No*		
More Difficult and/or More Expensive to Raise Capital	33.3%	30.8%	35.9%	19.7%	31.1%	49.2%	2	2.731 (.2553)
Reduction in Investment in Developing Stages	30.6	22.2	47.2	12.7	20.0	67.3	2	5.022 (.0812)

Appendix B. Table 6. Other Potential Effects

Questions 6, 4, 3, 2 and 8	Responses: Firms with < $10mm Sales			Responses: Firms with > $10mm Sales			Tests for Differences	
							df	χ²
Change in Closeness of Benefits from R & D Projects	*Nearer* 50.0%	*Longer* 13.9%	*Neither* 36.1%	*Nearer* 34.8%	*Longer* 30.3%	*Neither* 34.8%	2	3.902 (.1422)
Change in Risk of R & D Projects	*More* 4.0	*Less* 44.0	*Neither* 52.0	*More* 5.0	*Less* 37.5	*Neither* 57.5	2	.280 (.8694)
Change in Yearly Variability of R & D	*More Variable* 48.8	*More Stable* 9.3	*No Change* 41.9	*More Variable* 15.6	*More Stable* 11.7	*No Change* 72.7	2	15.502 (.0004)
Change in R & D Proposal Completion Time	*No Change* 2.5	*Probably Decreased* 6.3	*Probably Increased* 31.3	*No Change* 63.8	*Probably Decreased* 7.2	*Probably Increased* 29.0	2	.075 (.9634)
Change of Classification of R & D	*Yes* 2.2	*No* 97.8		*Yes* 6.6	*No* 93.4		1	.434 (.5102)
Change in Method of Tax Reporting for R & D	*Change* 21.7	*No Change* 78.3		*Change* 3.8	*No Change* 96.2		1	8.057 (.0045)

Chapter IX

Impact of R & D Rule on the Level and Variability of R & D Expenditures

Based upon the hypotheses described in Chapter IV and the evidence of Chapter VIII, further analysis of the impact of FAS 2 is clearly suggested. This chapter presents the results of tests designed to determine whether there was an association between the time that FAS 2 (ASR 178 of the SEC) became effective in 1975 and changes in the levels of R & D expenditures of deferral firms relative to those of expense firms. Also reported are the results of tests for changes in the variability of R & D expenditures after FAS 2 took effect.

A. SAMPLE DESCRIPTION

Because the hearings revealed that small, high-technology firms opposed an expense-only rule and were the primary users of the deferral method, the sample of treatment (deferral) firms was confined to firms which had securities traded over-the-counter. The sample was selected from the *Disclosure Journal*. Each firm had to have an auditor's qualification for the mandated switch in 1975 (or 1974 for early compliers) from deferral to expense, indicating that there was a material effect on profit as a result of the switch.[1]

Although Rule 2 did not become binding until 1975, firms that made switches in 1974 also were selected because it was assumed that some companies decided to switch in 1974 after

Table IX.1. Treatment and Control Samples

Treatment	Industry SIC	CONTROL (Match)	Industry SIC
Addmaster	(3573)	Anderson Jacobson Inc.	(3573)
AFA Protective Systems	(7393)	Market Facts Inc.	(7399)
Allen Organ	(3931)	Ivac Corp.	(3841)
Andersen 2000	(3881)	Intercontinental Dynam	(3811)
Andersen Labs Inc.	(3573)	Computer Consoles	(3573)
Aspen Systems	(7372)	Datatab Inc.	(7370)
Buck Engineering	(3825)	Qonaar Corp.	(3820)
Butler National Corp.	(3449) (3662)	Solid State Scientific	(3679)
Cetrol Electronics Corp.	(3673)	Physio Control Corp.	(3699)
Chattem Drug & Chemical	(2830)	Information Internat'l	(3830)
Coleman American	(6711)	Waters Instrument Inc.	(3699)
Compucorp	(3570)	Hunt Manufacturing	(3570)
Comtech Labs Inc.	(3662)	Communications Industry	(3662)
Cordis Dow Corp.	(3841)	Extracorporeal Medical	(3841)
CPT	(3570)	Computer Products	(3573)
Datascope	(3699)	Nicolet Instruments	(3699)
DBA Systems	(7372)	Nat'l Data Communicat.	(7370)
Dewey Electronics	(3573)	Advanced Micro Devices	(3670)
Digi-Log Systems	(3573)	Comten Inc.	(3573)
Educational Development	(2731) (3652)	Radiation Dynamics Inc.	(3662)
Electric Regulator	(3622)	Altair Corp.	(3662)
Electro-Catheter	(3841)	U.S. Surgical Corp.	(3846)
Fabri-Tek	(3573)	Universal Instruments	(3550)
General Data Comm.	(3661)	Farinon Corp.	(3661)
Graham Magnetics	(3449) (3679)	Siliconix Inc.	(3679)
Graphic Scanning Corp.	(7399)	Horizons Research	(7399)
Hygain Electronics	(3662)	ESL Inc.	(3573)
Industrial Nucleonics	(7370)	Comshare Inc.	(7370)
Kalvar Corp.	(3861)	Pako Corp.	(3861)
Mor-Flo Industries	(3630)	Rival Manufacturing	(3630)
New Brunswick	(3811)	Gelman Instruments	(3811)
Optical Radiation	(3640)	Aerotron Inc.	(3662)
REM Metals	(3540)	Scherr-Tumico Inc.	(3540)
Schaevitz Engineering	(3811)	Hach Chemical Co.	(3811)
Sensormatic Electronics	(3662)	Resdel Industries	(3662)
Specialty Composites	(3079)	Eberline Instrument Co.	(3823)
SRC Labs Inc.	(3673) (3499)	United Mcgill Corp.	(3499)
Staco Inc.	(3612)	Woodhead (Daniel) Inc.	(3699)
T-Bar Inc.	(3679)	Vitramon Inc.	(3679)
Technical Communications	(3573)	Beehive Internat'l	(3573)
Thetford	(3589)	Acme General Corp.	(3499)
Transidyne General	(3841)	Survival Technology	(3841)
Visual Sciences	(5084)	Analog Devices	(3679)

knowledge of the Board's decision was made public in October 1974. Thus, later reference made to "prior" and "post" periods indicates before or after the switch (1974 or 1975 depending on the company) rather than before or after 1975. Also, only companies whose Form 10–Ks were available and whose reports disclosed sufficient data during the 1970–1977 period on R & D outlays and other items necessary to perform the statistical tests described below were selected. The final treatment sample consisted of 43 companies.[2]

A matched group of 43 control companies, which had been expensing prior to FAS 2 and therefore were unaffected by the rule, was then selected from a list of approximately 800 companies traded over-the-counter. An effort was made to select a match for each treatment firm which was similar with respect to several critical variables during the pre-rule period. In particular, a company-to-company match was made on the basis of the following variables measured over the 1970–1975 period: (1) firm size, as measured by sales; (2) R & D intensity, as measured by the ratio, R & D/Sales; (3) R & D growth; and (4) industry, as indicated by SIC code.[3] As in the case of the treatment firms, an additional criterion was that the necessary Form 10–K data be available for the 1970–1977 period. Table IX.1 contains a list of company names and SIC codes for treatment and control firms.

B. EMPIRICAL TESTS ON THE LEVEL OF R & D EXPENDITURES

The null hypothesis was that there was no change in the level and growth of R & D expenditures by treatment firms relative to control firms after the imposition of the rule mandating use of the expensing method. The alternative hypothesis was that R & D outlays and growth declined for treatment firms. These hypotheses were tested using nonparametric Wilcoxon matched-pairs signed-ranks tests.[4]

Nonparametric methods were selected because the majority of variables statistically examined had widely dispersed distributions with a significant number of outlier observations. Such observations could invalidate results obtained using parametric tests. Because nonparametric techniques rely on ordinal ranking procedures, and thereby place less emphasis on outliers, it was possible to include these observations in the analysis.

The statistical results and definitions of test variables used to measure reductions in R & D are provided in Table IX.2. Table IX.3 contains the computed values of the test variables for each of the nine tests conducted.

The first test variable, the mean of the annual percent change in R & D (%ΔR&D) was computed for each of the treatment (deferral) companies for both prior and post Rule 2 periods. The Wilcoxon test was then used to examine the set of 43 company differences between prior and post observations.[5] The purpose of the test was to ascertain whether there was a systematic reduction in %ΔR&D across firms subsequent to Rule 2.

Next, the necessary computations were performed for a similar test on the control (expense) sample to determine whether there was a systematic reduction in %ΔR&D for these companies. Lastly, the difference between each prior and post observation in the control group was subtracted from the difference between each prior and post observation of its match in the treatment group, and the same analysis was applied to these (joint) differences.

Examination of the joint differences for the matched pairs provided a means of partially controlling for other unspecified events that influenced the levels of R & D expenditures during the test period, while simultaneously detecting changes in the location of the %ΔR&D variable for the deferral firms relative to expense firms.[6] More specifically, it may be noted that the Wilcoxon matched-pairs test on differences does not require that the distribution of differences be the same for separate pairs. Also, the test does not preclude the possibility that R & D expenditures are correlated both before and after the rule for a particular firm, and between treatment and control firms. This assumption is critical since R & D expenditure levels may have been affected by similar exogenous variables such as credit availability and other regulations.

The results of the 3 tests described above are presented in the first row of Table IX.2. Section (a) indicates that there was a significant reduction in %ΔR&D after FAS 2 for the treatment companies. Section (b) indicates that this was not the case for

Table IX.2. Results of Wilcoxon Matched-Pairs Signed-Ranks for Reduction in R & D Expenditures

Test Variable	DEFERRAL (a) Prior Period–Post Period					EXPENSE (b) Prior Period–Post Period					JOINT: DEFERRAL - EXPENSE (c)=(a)-(b)				
	n	+ ranks (mean)	− ranks (mean)	z-score		n	+ ranks (mean)	− ranks (mean)	z-score		n	+ ranks (mean)	− ranks (mean)	z-score
$\overline{\%\Delta R\&D}$	43	26 (25.58)	17 (16.53)	2.318***		43	15 (23.33)	28 (21.29)	−1.485		43	26 (24.38)	17 (18.35)	1.944**
$\overline{R\&D/Sales}$	43	31 (24.65)	12 (15.17)	3.514****		43	19 (22.26)	24 (21.79)	−.604		43	30 (24.80)	13 (15.54)	3.272***
$\overline{R\&D/Y+R\&D}$	43	24 (24.54)	18 (17.44)	1.719**		43	26 (22.15)	17 (21.76)	1.244		43	25 (22.96)	18 (20.67)	1.220

Test Variable	n	+ ranks (mean)	− ranks (mean)	z-score
$\overline{R\&D_D/R\&D_{D+E}}$	43	35 (22.34)	3 (20.50)	3.731****

Variable Definitions:

$\overline{\%\Delta R\&D}$ = average % change in Research and Development (R&D)

$\overline{R\&D/Sales}$ = average ratio of R&D to Sales

$\overline{R\&D/Y+R\&D}$ = average ratio of R&D to Income Before R&D

$\overline{R\&D_D/R\&D_{D+E}}$ = average ratio of R&D of deferral firm to total R&D of that firm and its match

Notes:
One Tail Tests
* significant at the .10 level
** significant at the .05 level
*** significant at the .01 level
**** significant at the .001 level

143

Table IX.3. Test Variable Observations

Case	$\overline{\%\Delta R\&D}_{Prior-Post}$			$\overline{\dfrac{R\&D_D}{R\&D_{D+E}}}_{Prior-Post}$	$\overline{R\&D/Sales}_{Prior-Post}$			$\overline{R\&D/(Y+R\&D)}_{Prior-Post}$		
	Deferral (D)	Expense (E)	Joint		Deferral (D)	Expense (E)	Joint	Deferral (D)	Expense (E)	Joint
1	.66699	−.08592	.75292	.16217	−.01096	.02853	−.03949	−.63758	.14979	−.78738
2	−.79823	−.08854	−.70969	.17433	.00687	−.00454	.01141	.23952	−.10198	.34149
3	1.80538	−.33413	2.13951	−.01073	.00542	.03764	−.03222	.11070	.51415	−.40345
4	−.01120	−.03988	.02868	.17620	.12226	−.00406	.12632	.54074	.11621	.42453
5	−.76328	−.29324	−.47004	.20653	−.00791	−.06438	.05647	.24959	−.07825	.32783
6	2.90442	−.05292	2.95734	.02211	.00729	−.00177	.00906	.54827	.01681	.53146
7	.07265	.71444	−.64179	.23619	.00101	−.01926	.02028	−.02710	−.52107	.49398
8	.41209	1.09024	−.67815	.03477	1.31239	−.06061	1.37300	−.07638	−.16487	.08849
9	.40368	.37395	.02973	.04471	.00249	−.00238	.00487	.06726	−.05245	.11971
10	−.61011	−.28324	−.32687	−.05582	−.00622	.16494	−.17116	−.13173	.18430	−.31602
11	2.93343	−.07108	3.00451	−.02607	.05740	.00087	.05653	−.13726	.27335	−.41061
12	−.07204	−.12293	.05089	.10399	−.06201	.00023	−.06224	−.15902	.00455	−.16358
13	4.29438	−.70100	4.99538	−.07445	−.00001	.00386	.00385	.01810	−.02217	.04027
14	−.15500	.05142	−.20642	.14901	.59304	−.01921	.61225	.51122	−.27712	.78834
15	6.12334	−.07845	6.20179	−.23706	−.02218	−.00483	−.01735	.20966	.11072	.09893
16	.53110	.34396	.18714	−.10573	−.01886	−.00489	−.01398	−.09177	−.05912	−.03265
17	.09632	.14071	−.04439	.05933	.00870	−.12892	.13762	−.11904	.09014	−.20918
18	−4.16335	−.13259	−4.03076	.07604	.03689	−.01225	.04914	−.21861	.05006	−.26866
19	1.29552	−.46108	1.75661	.09463	.24998	.12255	.12742	.58583	.13568	.45015

144

20	−.14055	.31786	−.45841	.17405	.03690	−.01059	.04750	−.07023	.01043	−.08067
21	−.16909	.73454	−.90363	.01101	.00887	.02669	−.01781	−.19325	.34726	−.54051
22	1.67934	−.31519	1.99453	.09687	−.01254	.00717	−.01970	−.00423	.19224	−.19647
23	.29532	1.16375	−.86843	.35388	.07654	−.00889	.08543	−.17712	−.08806	−.08906
24	.30983	−.99192	1.30175	.17230	.55092	.00019	.55072	.35102	−.30623	.65724
25	.51564	−.12154	.63718	.02496	−.00288	−.00041	−.00247	−.09781	.06604	−.16385
26	7.87496	−.19459	8.06955	−.23918	−.01108	−.00472	−.00636	−.16935	−.26822	.09887
27	−.22869	.07270	−.30139	.00657	.01328	−.00400	.01728	.38455	−.00067	.38388
28	.25491	−.32320	.57811	.00149	−.02606	.01695	−.04301	−.43945	.37294	−.81239
29	−.14682	−.49164	.34483	.20977	.07704	−.01065	.08769	.00000	−.09058	.09058
30	.18424	−.16273	.34696	.16217	.00395	.00272	.00123	.06610	.03684	.02926
31	.23988	.16758	.07231	.44224	.03516	−.01321	.04836	.07125	.39067	−.31942
32	1.17363	−.31191	1.48555	.03011	.01681	.00857	.00824	.12124	.23507	−.11384
33	.35334	−.12667	.48000	.00176	.01268	.00244	.01024	−.08589	.17846	−.26434
34	−.07627	−.06103	−.01524	.13505	.02763	.00307	.02456	.34120	−.06598	.40717
35	−.79877	−.14063	−.65814	.13262	.27823	.00196	.27627	.52257	.00139	.52117
36	.17675	.10341	.07334	.08520	.15064	−.01144	.16207	.41812	.20000	.21812
37	.56667	−5.43684	6.00352	.28956	.45184	−.00640	.45824	.51629	−.10757	.62386
38	−.52298	.02370	−.54668	.02946	.00040	.00596	−.00557	.07854	.05866	.01988
39	−.26047	−.65967	.39920	.01378	.01694	−.01065	.02759	.50480	.17375	.33105
40	−.34443	−.17333	−.17111	.22116	.30759	.06267	.24492	.59262	.32652	.26610
41	.26066	−1.53650	1.79716	−.06675	−.00636	−.00594	−.00041	.05536	−.07295	.12832
42	−.16021	.44300	−.60322	.07442	.25876	.14285	.11590	.14264	−.60512	.74776
43	4.97271	.12365	4.84906	.13328	.13040	.00633	.12407	−.10861	−.01073	−.09788

Note: Variable definitions are provided in Table IX-2.

the control companies, and section (c) indicates that when the treatment and control company results are considered jointly, the reduction for the deferral companies remains significant.

As shown in Table IX.2, three additional variables were examined using a similar approach as that described for %ΔR&D. These variables were the ratio R&D/Sales, the ratio R&D/ Income before R & D, and the ratio of R & D of the deferral company to the total of R & D of the same company plus the R & D of its match (expense) company.

Overall, the results for the deferral companies indicate that the association between the passage of FAS 2 (ASR 178) and a decline in each of the test variables is significant. The joint results examining the time series of the differences between companies from the two groups is also significant except for one measure.[7,8] Thus, almost all measures used point to a significant association between a relative decline of R & D expenditures for the deferral group and the imposition of the new measurement rule.

The test variable or measure most commonly used to measure R & D changes is R&D/Sales, or research intensity. According to the National Science Foundation the ratio of company sponsored R&D/Sales for manufacturing has remained fairly constant between 1964 and 1977 (*Mosaic,* 1979). Table IX.2 shows that there is a highly significant association between the passage of FAS 2 and a relative decline in R&D/Sales for the companies forced to switch. The probability of such a relative decline occurring by chance is 1 in 1,000.

Figure IX.1 illustrates the change in the median value of R&D/Sales for the deferral and expense groups over the 1971–1977 period.[9] It clearly shows a relative change in the ratio between the two groups between 1974 and 1975. (It will be recalled that about 50 percent of the deferral companies switched after October 1974 in anticipation of the January 1, 1975 mandate).

In sum, the results of Table IX.2 which are concerned with the actual changes in the level of R & D expenditures are consistent with the survey results presented in Chapter VIII, i.e., they suggest a significant reduction in R & D by affected firms around 1975. In fact, taken together they seem to point to the

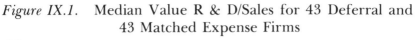

Figure IX.1. Median Value R & D/Sales for 43 Deferral and 43 Matched Expense Firms

expense-only rule as the cause of the relative decline in the levels of R & D by the deferral companies.

C. HYPOTHESES RELATED TO VARIABILITY

Even if there were no reductions in R & D outlays associated with the impact of Rule 2, it is possible that changes in R & D investment behavior would be manifest through an alteration of the variability of the outlays. The survey results reported in Chapter VIII did indicate significant differences between deferral and expense company responses and between the responses of companies with less than $10 million of sales and over $10 million of sales regarding the variability of outlays (question 4 of the survey). These results suggested that perhaps Rule 2 affected the pattern of R & D expenditures.

Several statements by organizations or committees concerned

with the measuring and reporting problems of R & D offer interesting insights into the importance attached to the relationship between R & D expenditures and a firm's income stream. The Financial Executives Institute, mostly composed of chief financial executives of large corporations, responded to the FASB's Discussion Memorandum on accounting for R & D expenditures by noting that development costs often fluctuate widely between years and that capitalization and subsequent amortization would give more meaningful reports (Financial Executives Institute, 1974).[10]

Other committees were formed by the Assistant Secretary for Science and Technology of the Commerce Department to examine numerous approaches for stimulating R & D activity in the U.S. economy. Among the concerns of a committee of representatives of small, high-technology firms to the Commerce Technical Advisory Board was the instability of small business R & D expenditures. It stated and recommended that:

> Stability in R & D activity in small firms would be encouraged if such firms were allowed to establish and replenish a Reserve for Research and Development in better profit years to be used to stabilize R & D in lower profit or loss years. The reserve would allow the firm to retain more earnings, which is important to firms seeking credit and investment (*Recommendations*, 1978, p. 31).

One of the implications of this recommendation is that actual outlays are needlessly high in profitable years and low in unprofitable years and that the use of an accounting reserve would lead to greater stability of the R & D expense over the cycle so that R & D outlays could be made with less concern for the effect on profit. The deferral or capitalization method, prior to its elimination, tended to perform the function of leveling the expenses. Thus, an implication of the recommendation is that removal of the deferral option would affect the variability of R & D expenditures.

From the above discussion, two possibilities are suggested. The use of deferral prior to the expense-only rule allowed more variable outlays since the amortization process would ensure a less variable effect on income. Variability of R & D expenditures would then be less after the rule because of the higher correlation between the period's expenditure and the period's net income which would be necessary to achieve the same pattern of income obtained prior to the rule.

Another possibility is that variability of R & D expenditures increased after the rule became effective. The FASB recognized that the imposition of the rule, *ceteris paribus,* would increase the variability of income since R & D expenditures would no longer be "smoothed" through the amortization process. Asserting that risk is correlated with the variability of earnings, in support of the expense-only rule, the Board stated that ". . . in assessing risk, financial statement users have indicated that they seek information about the variability of earnings" (FAS 2, par. 50). However, an additional random element is introduced if, as was suggested in both the oil and gas and R & D hearings, the pattern of R & D investment expenditures would be changed when Statement 2 became effective in order to reduce what might otherwise be more variable earnings. This could lead to more stability in expenditures as a substitute for the amortization process, but it is also possible that R & D expenditures would be more variable as a "manipulative" tool to offset any other factors leading to income variability.

D. EMPIRICAL RESULTS ON VARIABILITY OF R & D EXPENDITURES

The null hypothesis tested was that there was no change in variability. The alternate hypothesis was that there was either an increase or decrease in variability. Because the time series of the pre- and post-periods were short (4 years or less), it would not have been meaningful to use a measure of variation based upon standard deviation. The three test measures of variability that were selected are shown in Table IX.4 along with the results and their levels of significance. The test measures presented in Table IX.4 are confined to absolute values of actual changes.[11]

Although the deferral companies alone exhibit significant or highly significant changes in variability (Table IX.4), the joint differences of deferral minus expense companies show significance at the .01 level for only one test measure, the absolute value of the actual change of R&D/Sales. Nevertheless, for all three measures of the joint differences, the results for the

Table IX.4.   Results of Wilcoxon Matched-Pairs Signed-Ranks Tests for Change in Variability of R&D Expenditure Pattern

| Test Variable | *DEFERRAL* (a) Prior Period–Post Period | | | | *EXPENSE* (b) Prior Period–Post Period | | | | *JOINT: DEFERRAL-EXPENSE* | | | |
	n	+ ranks (mean)	– ranks (mean)	z score	n	+ ranks (mean)	– ranks (mean)	z score	n	+ ranks (mean)	– ranks (mean)	z score
|actual Δ in % Δ RD|	40	28 (23.43)	12 (13.67)	3.307****	41	27 (21.57)	14 (21.57)	1.665*	39	22 (23.09)	17 (16.06)	1.647*
|actual Δ in RD/Sales|	43	36 (24.81)	7 (7.57)	5.071****	43	27 (24.07)	16 (18.50)	2.137**	43	29 (23.90)	14 (18.07)	2.656***
|actual Δ in RD/Y+RD|	43	27 (22.44)	15 (19.80)	1.932**	43	23 (24.13)	20 (19.55)	.990	43	25 (22.92)	18 (20.72)	1.207

Note:

Two Tail Tests
*   significant at the .10 level
**   significant at the .05 level
*** significant at the .01 level
**** significant at the .001 level

Variable Definitions:

\|actual Δ in % Δ RD\| = mean of the absolute value of the actual yearly change in the percentage of RD.

\|actual Δ in RD/Sales\| = mean of the absolute value of the actual yearly change in RD/Sales.

\|actual Δ in RD/Y+RD\| = mean of the absolute value of the actual yearly change in RD to Income before RD.

number of positive and negative ranks are in the direction that indicate a greater decline in R & D variability for deferral companies over expense companies after the imposition of the expense-only rule. On balance, therefore, the results are suggestive but weak and the null hypothesis of no change in the variability of outlays cannot be rejected.

E. SUMMARY AND CONCLUDING REMARKS

Based upon the results of (1) statistical tests of the association of FAS 2, *Accounting for Research and Development Costs* (ASR 178 of the SEC) with reductions in the level of R & D expenditures of affected firms and (2) the responses to a questionnaire by key financial managers discussed in the preceding chapter, it may be concluded that the empirical evidence supports the premise that the expense-only rule caused a relative decline in R & D expenditures for small, high-technology firms which had previously used the deferral method of measurement. The only previous empirical study on the direct consequences of Statement 2 was a Commerce Department Survey about which strong reservations were expressed in Chapter VI.

It cannot be concluded from the R & D study that FAS 2 should be suspended, as was done for FAS 19, since there has been no assessment of the benefits that were alleged to occur as a result of the enhancement of comparability through increased uniformity. For as the FASB has said, in describing its own activities:

> What [the Board] can do when considering a proposed standard is to identify and weigh, however subjectively, the possible immediate costs and benefits to preparers and users; determine whether the standard passes that first cost-benefit test and reject it if it does not; then, if the standard passes that test, consider any costs imposed on and benefits reaped by other parts of the economy that might modify that initial judgement (Exposure Draft, 1979, par. 123).

The background material and the evidence presented in this chapter suggest that the cost associated with the relative reduction of R & D outlays of small, high-technology firms may have been ignored.[12] Just as the SEC and the FASB have given more attention in the 1970s to the impact of disclosure rules on small firms, there may be a special need to evaluate the consequences to small firms of uniformity mandated in any measurement rule. Moreover, the fact that small, high-technology firms have an important role in the innovation process suggests that, based upon the evidence provided above, perhaps, special attention should be given to the R & D measurement problem.

NOTES

1. Since FAS 2 was dated October 1974, it is likely that early compliers had a fiscal closing date between October and December 31, 1974. Compliance prior to October 1974 would have been considered a "cumulative change in accounting principle" (APB 20) and would have led to larger decreases in profit than compliance after October 1974 because of the necessity to write-off the capitalized value of R & D to profit. Compliance with FAS 2 after October 1974 required that capitalized R & D be written off as a direct charge to retained earnings, i.e., as "a prior period adjustment."

2. No firm in this group had sales exceeding $100 million and about 50 percent switched in 1974.

3. If after matching on the first three variables, a four digit SIC industry match was available, it was selected. Twenty-four pairs were matched on this basis. The industry matches for the remaining nineteen cases were less perfect. Tests on subsets of the paired sample indicate that the results reported below are not sensitive to how close pairs within the sample were matched by industry.

4. The Wilcoxon test has a high power-efficiency relative to other procedures designed specifically for the matched-pair situation. Its asymtotic efficiency, as compared to the t-test, is 95.5% for large samples in appropriate circumstances (95% for small samples). It is generally regarded as the best of the order tests for two samples and may be superior to the t-test when appropriate assumptions for that test are not met (Hollander and Wolfe, p. 82).

5. To perform the analysis the differences between %ΔR&D prior and %ΔR&D post were rank ordered in terms of their absolute size. If there was no systematic differences, (%ΔR&D prior–%ΔR&D post) would be expected to be distributed symmetrically around zero. Equivalently, the sum of the ranks of the positive differences would be expected to be equal to the sum of the ranks of the negative differences.

6. As previously mentioned, the closeness of percentage changes in R & D (R & D growth) between treatment and control companies in the prior period was one of the variables that was considered in selecting matches.

7. Two factors may account for the lack of significance of the variable R&D/Income before R & D, although the direction of the change is consistent with the other results. First, the stability of the ratio varies depending upon the proximity of the denominator to zero, and the ratio was defined as 1 when income before R & D was negative. Second, among industrial companies where income before R & D was positive, the variation in this variable was

extremely large. For example, the computer industry for 1977 showed average percent of R & D to final income equal to 54 percent (*Business Week*, July 3, 1978); one company had an average of more than 6,000 percent and another had an average of 10 percent. The R&D/Sales ratio, on the other hand, exhibited small variations around the mean.

8. Because it was difficult to control for all variables in the matching process, joint tests were repeated using the Mann-Whitney test. Like the Wilcoxon test, the Mann-Whitney test is a two sample test which considers both the order and magnitude of variables but does not recognize matched pairs. The significance levels for the two joint variables %ΔR&D and R&D/Sales were .015 and .003, respectively. As was the case for the Wilcoxon test, the last variable, R&D/(Y + RD), was insignificant at the .10 level. Also, in order to test the sensitivity of our results to the precision of our matches, all ten tests described in Table IX.2 were replicated on ten subsets of paired samples. Subsets were selected which met the following criteria for the difference between a treatment and its match firm in the pre-FAS 2 period: (1) difference in average sales < $5 million; (2) average growth of sales, as measured by %ΔSales, greater for treatment firm; (3) average growth of sales greater for control firm; (4) difference in average R&D/Sales < .02; (5) difference in variability of R&D/Sales < .01, and five combinations of these criteria. In all cases, the results were consistent with those reported in Table IX.2, although the significance levels changed slightly from one case to another.

9. 1970 was excluded because some control companies did not report 1970 data for R & D expenditures.

10. Although the predominant membership of the Financial Executive Institute comes from large companies, a very high percentage of which expensed prior to Rule 2, the position of the Institute was that a standard for R & D "should permit reasonable variations to reflect underlying circumstances."

11. Similar tests were performed using absolute values of *percentage* changes. The results for those variables were consistent with those reported below and therefore have not been detailed in the Tables.

12. The Advisory Committee recommended that the SEC consider whether the "quality and amount of information" is cost effective and, specifically, whether issuers find it more difficult to innovate (*Report of the Advisory Committee*, 1977, p. 317). Yet, ASR 178 did not mention the costs and benefits of the expense-only rule for R & D, although in a previous release of only a few months, it was asserted in ASR 177 that the benefits of interim reporting substantially outweighed the costs, except for small companies.

Chapter X

The Relationship Between Firm Characteristics and the Choice of Financial Measurement Methods: An Application to R & D

As discussed in Chapter II, since the formation of the SEC in 1933 there has been a continual debate over whether firms should be free to choose among alternative measurement methods for external reporting or whether measurement methods should be uniform across all firms. Nevertheless, little attention has been given to the differences between firms which select different reporting methods when choices are available. Although in 1966 Sorter, et al., investigated the relationship between external reporting choice and management styles, only recently have authors attempted to explain the relationship between the financial measurement choices of firms and their financial and operating characteristics (Deakin, 1979; Dhaliwal, 1980; Hagerman and Zmijewski, 1979; Watts and Zimmerman, 1978). Knowledge of these relationships has become increasingly important as the FASB and the SEC have placed greater emphasis on the elimination of choice in financial disclosure and measurement.

The purpose of this chapter is to present the results of a study which sought to determine what differences existed between the characteristics (circumstances) of firms which had chosen to use the deferral method of measuring R & D prior to 1975 and firms which had chosen to expense R & D at that time. FAS 2 prohibited the use of the deferral method after January 1, 1975.

An important policy question is whether dissimilarities in firm characteristics should preclude the use of a single reporting method. Addressing this question, Burton (1976) has stated that accounting principles should recognize "the need for differing treatment of different factual circumstances, and not lay down rules so rigid as to force unlike entities into the same reporting model."

As reported below, there is some evidence which indicates that firms affected by FAS 2 (those that previously had used the deferral method) were significantly dissimilar from their expensing counterparts. Furthermore, the evidence in Chapters VIII and IX suggests that the rule may have had an adverse effect on the R & D investment decisions of deferral firms.

It is important to ask, therefore, what were the differences between deferral and expensing firms, how might those differences have affected their accounting measurement choice, and could those differences have explained a possible negative effect when the deferral method was banned? The answers to these questions are relevant to the verification and extension of existing theories of accounting choice. In addition, an understanding of the reasons why companies voluntarily select measurement rules is relevant to the ongoing evaluation of the costs and benefits of uniformity. Finally, such a study may provide useful insights into an important public policy question concerning the effects of FASB (SEC) regulations on those small firms having significant R & D outlays, i.e., "high technology" or "research intensive" firms. Although the study reported in this chapter is limited to a description of the differences in firm characteristics without developing a theory, it is hoped that its results, together with existing and future work, will provide insights leading to the development and verification of a positive theory of measurement choice.

The next section of this chapter briefly reviews the literature on accounting choice and summarizes the R & D measurement issue and related evidence. This is followed by a description of the sample, variable selection process and data sources. Next, the results of univariate and multivariate tests for differences in the characteristics of firms which had chosen alternative reporting methods are presented. The final section provides a summary and concluding remarks.

A. RELATED STUDIES

Watts and Zimmerman (1978) postulate that taxes, regulation, management compensation plans, information production costs and political costs are critical factors in determining management's attitude toward particular accounting standards. Consideration of these factors leads to a model in which support or opposition to a particular standard or method of reporting is related to firm size.

In particular, Watts and Zimmerman hypothesize that large firms generally will be supportive of methods which reduce reported earnings because for such firms, the regulatory and political cost savings associated with those methods will dominate other considerations. Contrarily, small firms are expected to be more concerned with the impact of reporting rules on information production costs and management compensation plans than with political or regulatory factors which, for them, are relatively unimportant. Accordingly, these firms would tend to lobby against income-reducing reporting methods. Evidence of this behavior is presented by Watts and Zimmerman in a study of the differences in the lobbying positions of small and large companies with respect to the public hearings on general price level accounting prior to FAS 33.

Hagerman and Zmijewski (1979) explore the effect of other firm variables including systematic risk, capital intensity and concentration on a firm's preference for accounting principles. They theorize that when earnings are higher than expected, political and regulatory costs will be an increasing function of the values of those variables. As a consequence, they reason that firms with relatively high values for those variables will prefer accounting methods which tend to reduce income. The results of their empirical work, however, do not indicate that these factors are consistent determinants of firm preference.

Finally, Deakin (1979) and Dhaliwal (1980) empirically tested whether there were differences in the operating and financial characteristics of firms using different measurement methods in the oil and gas industry. Deakin's study focused on whether the choice of full cost (FC) or successful efforts (SE) accounting could be predicted on the basis of several firm characteristics including aggressiveness in exploration activities, size, age and dependency on external capital, whereas Dhaliwal limited his work to examining whether the FC–SE choice was related to differences in financial structures.

The univariate results of the Deakin study indicate significant differences between the two groups, with FC companies generally being younger, having greater leverage and greater capital expenditures per dollar of revenues. Moreover, using a discriminant analysis model he finds that "one may distinguish between full cost and successful efforts companies" at the .01 significance level although "the differences between companies explained by the model represent only a small portion of the total differences between companies" (Deakin, 1979, p. 729). Nevertheless, Deakin concludes that important differences exist between FC and SE firms.

Using multiple measures of financial leverage and controlling for differences in size, Dhaliwal also finds that FC firms are more highly levered than their successful efforts counterparts. This supports his hypothesis that a more highly levered firm will select the FC method in order to report higher values of assets, equity and earnings and thereby make protective covenants in its debt agreements less restrictive.

The work of Deakin and Dhaliwal is particularly relevant to the investigation of the relationship between choice in R & D measurement and firm characteristics reported in this chapter. This is because the choice of measurement for exploration and development costs prior to FAS 19, *Accounting and Reporting for Oil and Gas Producing Companies,* was similar in many ways to the choice that existed for measuring R & D outlays prior to FAS 2. Likewise, the controversy surrounding both rules during the hearings on their respective exposure drafts was similar.

In each case, the choice was one of using a deferral (capitalization) method or using an expense method to measure an expenditure. In each case, the FASB had proposed to eliminate the deferral alternative. Critics of the FASB's decision in both instances claimed that there existed significant differences between the characteristics (circumstances) of those companies which had been deferring and those expensing, and that because of these differences, both methods should be permitted. Also suggested was that exploration and development (R & D) outlays would be substantially reduced if FAS 19 (FAS 2) was adopted. Below, the results of these latter two studies are compared to those relating to R & D choice.

B. VARIABLE SELECTION, SAMPLE COMPOSITION AND DATA SOURCES

The nine firm characteristics examined in this study are presented in Table X.1, together with the sixteen variables used to test for differences in these characteristics between R & D deferral and expensing firms. The decision to study each characteristic was based on the existing theory of firm choice (Gordon, 1964; Watts and Zimmerman, 1978), testimony at the hearings on the R & D rule in March 1974, and related empirical work on FAS 19 (Deakin, 1979; Dhaliwal, 1980). A discussion of each characteristic follows.

1. Firm Size

With respect to size, there existed prior evidence that firms which had selected the deferral method to report R & D were significantly smaller than those which had selected the expensing method. This evidence is detailed in Chapter VII.D. Also, an examination of the testimony at the March 1974 hearings before the FASB revealed that representatives of large companies generally supported the expensing rule, whereas objections to the rule were raised by small companies.[1,2]

Because it was apparent that relatively few large companies whose securities were traded on the major exchanges had been deferring R & D, the study was limited to smaller firms whose securities were traded-over-the-counter (OTC). For this population, however, size was still considered as an independent variable since it was desired to determine whether choice of reporting method and size were related within the OTC population. Inclusion of this variable in the analysis also permitted the screening out of any size effect which existed in order to isolate the effects of other explanatory variables.

Table X.1. Characteristics and Test Variables

Characteristics	Independent Variables			
I. Size	1. $\overline{\text{Sales}}$			
II. Variability of RD	2. $\left|\overline{\text{Actual } \Delta \text{ RD/Sales}}\right|$	3. $\overline{\left|\text{actual } \Delta \dfrac{\text{RD}}{(Y_{BT} + \text{RD})}\right|}$		
III. Growth of RD	4. RD/Sales growth			
IV. Profitability	5. $\overline{Y/\text{Sales}}$	6. $\overline{\text{NOI/TA}}$	7. $\overline{\text{RE/TA}}$	8. # years negative Y (1970–74)
V. Importance of RD	9. $\overline{\text{RD/Sales}}$	10. $\overline{\text{RD}/(Y_{BT} + \text{RD})}$		
VI. Sales and Earnings Growth	11. Sales (1968–1975)	12. EPS (1968–1975)		
VII. Dependence on External Capital	13. Funds Provided by Operations/ Capital Expenditures			
VIII. Leverage	14. $\overline{\dfrac{\text{Debt/Sales}}{\text{Assets—Intangibles}}}$	15. $\overline{\text{Debt/(Total}}$		
IX. Age	16. year incorp.			

VARIABLE
DEFINITIONS:

RD = Research and Development Expenditure
Y = Income
Y_{BT} = Income Before Tax
NOI = Net Operating Income

TA = Total Assets
RE = Retained Earnings
EPS = Earnings Per Share
Δ = Change

2. Variables Related to the Level and Volatility of Earnings

One of the primary concerns voiced by the deferral companies was the impact that Rule 2 would have on the level and volatility of their earnings streams.[3] Affected firms suggested that, if they were forced to expense R & D, reported earnings would decline and fluctuate more widely from year to year, and that these conditions would impair their ability to raise capital.[4]

As explained in Chapter IV, whether, in fact, the effect of the choice of accounting method on earnings and asset value would actually affect the firm's ability to raise capital is a separate issue, one of market efficiency. What is important here is only what management perceived would happen as a result of its choice of method. Thus, even if the capital markets were perfect in the sense of not being influenced by the change of reported numbers, managements of firms with growing and volatile R & D levels may have perceived that they would be affected, and, therefore, may have chosen the deferral method to increase earnings and lessen variability. Hence, the choice may have been deemed important by the preparer of the financial report irrespective of the effect on the user of the financial report (the stockholder or creditor).

Another reason that management might be opposed to a reporting method which produces greater earnings volatility relates to management compensation schemes which are often dependent on income levels (see Chapter IV.A). A survey by Watts and Zimmerman (1978, p. 116) of 52 firms indicated that 69 percent formally incorporated accounting income into their compensation plans. Hence, some managers might tend to select a method which smooths earnings to make their compensation less variable.

It should be noted that if a firm's yearly expenditures on R & D were constant, the level and variability of a firm's earnings would be unaffected by whether it chose to expense or defer R & D. However, for a firm whose expenditures on R & D were growing, choosing the expensing alternative would lead to lower earnings. Also, if a firm had highly variable R & D expenditures, the expensing alternative would lead to a greater variability of earnings. Hence, if the management of a firm with growing and volatile R & D desired to achieve a higher and smoother income stream, it would have been inclined to select the deferral method. Also, use of the deferral method in that case would lead to a greater book value for assets and stockholders' equity.

On the basis of the preceding analysis the variability and growth of R & D (measured by variables 2–4 in Table X.1) were included as explanatory characteristics. It was hypothesized that firms with high growth and firms with more variable R & D outlays were more likely to choose the deferral method. Also, it was hypothesized that firms with lower earnings levels (measured by variables 5–8) would be more concerned with the impact of the R & D measurement choice on earnings and therefore be inclined to select the deferral method.

3. R & D Intensity

In addition to being dependent on the variability of R & D and existing profit levels, the extent to which accounting choice will influence reported earnings and assets is also a function of the importance of the R & D activity in the firm. It is evident that the larger the proportion of the firm's activities (sales or earnings) devoted to R & D, *ceteris paribus,* the more likely expensing will produce lower asset, equity and income levels. Therefore, it was hypothesized that firms which are more research intensive would be more prone to select the deferral method. R & D intensity is measured by RD/Sales (variable 9) and $RD/(Y_{BT} + RD)$ (variable 10).[5]

4. Dependency on External Funds

Another factor which might have affected a firm's choice between deferring and expensing R & D was the reliance of that firm on external sources of funds. If a firm is heavily dependent upon external capital, it might be more concerned about externally reported numbers. This is particularly so if new capital is to be raised in the equity market, and if the suppliers of funds are primarily noninstitutional investors whose attention is more likely to be focused on the "bottom line."

The testimony of several investment bankers at hearings

conducted by the SEC in 1978 indicated that they believed that the capital markets for small growth firms are imperfect.[6] Specifically, they suggested that for such firms it could become more expensive and/or more difficult to raise capital because of lower income figures caused by changes in reporting methods. Perhaps the new equity markets are inefficient to some degree for small, OTC traded firms which are the subject of this study. Empirical evidence on this issue is scant.

For these reasons it is hypothesized that faster growing firms which are more dependent on external capital would choose to defer rather than to expense (variables 11 and 12). Also, the variable, Funds Provided by Operations/Capital Expenditures (variable 13) was included as a measure of a firm's dependence on external capital.

5. Financial Leverage and Age

Based on the empirical work of Deakin (1979) and Dhaliwal (1980) the degree of financial leverage also was hypothesized as a differentiating characteristic (variables 14 and 15).[7] As noted earlier, Deakin and Dhaliwal found that firms which selected the FC (deferral) method for reporting exploration and development costs in the oil and gas industry were more highly leveraged than SE firms. This finding is consistent with Dhaliwal's hypothesis that firms with higher debt levels are more concerned with reporting a greater book value of equity in order to make debt/equity constraints specified in loan agreements less restrictive. Because deferral treats R & D as an asset, the book value of equity would be greater under this method and therefore the debt/equity ratio lower.

The final characteristic considered is age of firm as indicated by year incorporated. It is hypothesized that a younger, developing stage company is more apt to defer R & D for financial reporting purposes in order to avoid large reported losses in beginning years when revenues are relatively low.

6. Sample and Data Selection Procedures

A preliminary list of 178 firms which deferred R & D prior to 1975 and which had equity securities traded over-the-counter was compiled from the May 1974–April 1975 and May 1975–April 1976 editions of the *Disclosure Journal.* Inclusion in the experimental sample of deferral firms required that (1) company data be available on the Compustat OTC file; and (2) the firms have an RD/Sales ratio greater than .01 and an RD/Income ratio greater than .05 for at least three years between 1970 and 1975. This screening process reduced the final deferral sample to 40 companies.

A group of companies which had been expensing prior to 1975 also was selected. As in the case of the deferral sample, these firms had to be listed on the Compustat OTC file and have ratios of RD/Sales greater than .01 and RD/Income greater than .05 for a minimum of three years during the 1970–1975 period. There were 152 firms that met these criteria. Approximately one third of these, 50 companies, were randomly selected as the final expense sample.[8] All the necessary data for the 90 sample firms were extracted from Compustat with the exception of year of incorporation which was obtained from Moody's OTC manual.[9] When available, data were used from the period 1968–1975 to compute the variability and growth variables and from the period 1970–1975 to compute means for the remaining variables.[10]

C. RESULTS OF UNIVARIATE AND MULTIVARIATE ANALYSES

1. Univariate Tests

To examine whether the deferral and expense firms differed with respect to the characteristics identified in the preceding section, first the median value of each variable was computed for each of the two samples. Median values for deferral and expense firms are shown in columns (2) and (4) of Table X.2. Column (3) contains the relationships which have been hypothesized between the two groups. The data suggest that the differences in the median values were in the expected direction for 13 of the 16 variables considered. The exceptions were the three growth variables: growth in sales, earnings and RD/Sales. In these cases, the expense firms had greater growth, on average, than deferral firms.

To determine whether the observed differences were significant, data from the two samples were pooled, firms were ranked according to the value of each variable, and a series of Mann-Whitney tests was performed. The null hypothesis was that no difference existed between the median values for deferral and expense firms.

The results of these tests are presented in Table X.2, columns (5) and (6). As signified by the significant Z scores, for 12 variables the null hypothesis was rejected at the .05 level; for another variable it was rejected at the .10 level. More importantly, the nature of the differences determined to be significant in these tests is consistent with the expected relationships indicated in column (3), again with the exception of variables 4, 11 and 12. As hypothesized, those firms that chose deferral had a more variable pattern of R & D and tended to be smaller, more R & D intensive, less profitable, more highly levered and incorporated a fewer number of years.

2. Multivariate Tests

In order to consider the interrelationships among variables and to simultaneously examine the ability of the entire variable set to discriminate between deferral and expense firms, further tests were conducted using multiple discriminant analysis (MDA). Because the objective of the study was to differentiate between two reporting groups, the appropriate form of the discriminant function was one dimensional and represented as:

$$Z = V_1X_1 + V_2X_2 + \ldots + V_nX_n$$

where: Z = Discriminant Score
X_i = Independent Variables
V_i = Discriminant Coefficients

The parameters of this function were estimated using a forward stepwise procedure. On the basis of the F ratio calculated by Rao's V-method, the procedure first selected the single variable best able to discriminate between the two groups of firms. The second and subsequent variables which entered the model were selected on the basis of their ability to improve the value of the discrimination criterion when combined with existing variables. At each step of the selection process previously selected

Table X.2. Medians and Results of Univariate and Multivariate Tests

(1)	(2) Deferral		Medians (3) Expected	(4) Expense		Mann-Whitney Statistics (5)	(6)	(7) Order of	Discriminant Coefficients (significant variables only) (8)	(9)	(10)
Test Variable	n	Median	Direction	n	Median	U	Z-Score	Entry	Unstandardized	Standardized	F Ratio
Size											
1. Sales	40	7.456	<	50	14.173	569.0	3.500****	3	−.01448	−.32006	6.72
Variability of RD											
2. Actual Δ RD/Sales	39	.015	>	50	.006	649.0	2.696***				
3. Actual Δ RD/Y$_{BT}$+RD	35	.228	>	45	.074	579.0	2.022**				
Growth of RD											
4. RD/Sales (1968–1975)	39	−.108	>	49	−.042	874.5	−.680				
Profitability											
5. Y/Sales	37	−.007	<	46	.038	565.0	2.620***				
6. NOI/Total Assets	37	.073	<	46	.134	535.0	2.895***				
7. RE/Total Assets	40	−.000	<	50	.000	585.0	3.370****				
8. # Years Negative Y	27	2.083	>	42	.375	322.0	3.165****				

	N			N							
Importance of RD											
9. RD/Sales	40	.058	>	50	.034	705.0	2.395***				
10. RD/Y_{BT}+RD)	37	.662	>	45	.301	466.5	3.411****	1	2.00484	.56355	11.23
Growth											
11. Sales	37	.163	>	49	.172	885.0	-.188				
12. Earnings	39	.015	>	50	.128	694.0	-2.324	2	-.15180	-.53552	7.98
Dependency on External Funds											
13. Funds Provided by Operations/ Capital Expenditures	40	.313	<	50	.548	706.5	2.383***	5	-.47853	-.25870	5.60
Leverage											
14. Debt/Sales	40	.147	>	50	.116	833.5	1.352*	4	-1.08455	-.30615	1.42
15. Debt/Total Assets	40	.139	>	50	.169	948.5	.418				
Age											
16. Year incorp.	37	65.000	>	49	60.000	687.5	1.915**				

Variable Definitions:

RD   Research and Development Expenditure
Y_{BT} Income Before Taxes
NOI   Net Operating Income
RE   Retained Earnings
Δ   Change

Notes:
One Tail Tests
*   Significant at the .10 level
**   Significant at the .05 level
***   Significant at the .01 level
****   Significant at the .001 level

variables were checked to determine whether their presence in the model remained significant at the .05 level when combined with the more recently selected variable. If a variable became insignificant, it was removed from the model.

Two-thirds of the sample firms were used to estimate the MDA function; the remaining third was used as a "hold out" sample to test the reliability of the model. Because of the high correlation among variables that were used to measure the same characteristic (see Table X.3) and because the estimation sample size was relatively small (60 firms), the number of variables entered into the discriminant program was limited to nine, one for each characteristic. The specific variables used to represent each of the nine characteristics were selected on the basis of the strength of the univariate results and the number of firms for which the necessary data were available.

The discriminant coefficients, F ratios, and order of entry for significant variables are presented in columns (7) through (10) of Table X.2. The 19.635 Chi-square statistic obtained for the five variable model is significant at the .001 level, indicating that the means for the deferral and expense groups clearly were different and came from different populations. Also, the model correctly classified 78.33 percent of sample companies into observed methods of reporting.[11]

The discriminant function assigned a lower score to firms that had chosen to expense R & D prior to 1975. Thus, the positive coefficients of the variable, $RD/(Y_{BT} + RD)$ and the negative coefficients for Sales and Funds Provided by Operations/Capital Expenditures are consistent with the hypothesized relationships, i.e., the more research intensive and smaller firms which were more dependent on external capital tended to be classified as firms which had selected the deferral method. Also consistent with the univariate results is the negative sign associated with earnings growth. Contrary to the earlier results, however, the sign of the leverage variable, Debt/Sales, was negative rather than positive as expected. The fact that this variable in a multivariate context provides different information may be attributed to its interrelationships with other variables.[12]

To determine the effectiveness of the MDA model, the firms of the "holdout" sample were classified into deferral and ex-

Table X.3. Correlations between Independent Variables

	Sales	RD/Sales	RD/(Y_{BT} + RD)	Y/Sales	NOI/TA	RE/TA	Debt/Sales
RD/(Y_{BT}+RD)		.69					
Y/Sales			-.68				
NOI/Sales			-.74	.80			
RE/TA		-.52	-.67	.76	.68		
Variability of RD/Sales	-52	.69	.73	-.60	-.58	-.69	
Debt/Sales				.50			
Funds Provided by Operations/ Capital Expenditures				.57	.54	.56	
Debt/Total Assets							.88

Note: Correlation coefficients reported only when ≥ .5 and significant at the .001 level.

pense firms on the basis of scores assigned by the discriminant function. The results indicate that 76.5 percent of the deferral firms and 77 percent of the expense firms were classified correctly, providing further evidence that the model generally was able to distinguish between deferral and expensing firms on the basis of selected financial and operating characteristics.

D. SUMMARY AND CONCLUDING REMARKS

The study reported in this chapter examined the differences between the characteristics of OTC firms which had selected to defer R & D and those which had chosen to expense. The univariate and multivariate analyses demonstrated that the two populations differed significantly with respect to several characteristics. This appeared to be confirmed by the predictive capability of the discriminant model. In general, the findings suggest that, when compared to firms that had chosen to use the expense method, firms which had been deferring prior to FAS 2 were smaller, less mature, less profitable, more highly levered, more highly dependent on external funds and more research intensive.

The findings reported here are similar to those found by Deakin (1979) in the analysis of characteristics of FC and SE firms; for he concluded that "discrimination can be supported on the basis of debt leverage and capital expenditure levels or on the basis of a combination of these two variables with measures of age and aggressiveness in exploration." The authors' results also are consistent with Dhaliwal's (1980) conclusion that FC firms are more highly levered than SE firms. Generalization to the generic choice between deferral and expensing, however, requires further research on other financial reporting methods.

Finally, two problems for future research are suggested by the results presented in this chapter and those in Chapters VIII and IX. First, when the differences in characteristics are as dissimilar as reported, it may be important to determine whether the imposition of a single measurement rule for R & D expenditures that is different from the one freely chosen can change the economic equilibrium of affected firms. Secondly, further consideration should be given to whether differences in firm characteristics are sufficiently important and identifiable to justify the use of dual measurement methods.

NOTES

1. This difference in behavior between large and small firms at the FASB hearings is consistent with Watts and Zimmerman's (1978) hypothesis.

2. The question as to why a significantly greater percentage of small firms capitalize as compared to large firms has not been answered. If R & D is evaluated from a portfolio point of view, rather than from a single project point of view as was done by the Board, on an economic basis one would expect an opposite distribution of methods. Large firms, taking advantage of diversification, could reduce the total risk of the R & D portfolio thus reducing uncertainty and making the benefits of the portfolio easier to predict, leading them to defer (Bierman and Dukes, 1975).

3. A reasonable assumption stemming from the objections of small, deferral companies which were concerned about the impact of FAS 2 on the variability of their earnings is that the variability of their R & D expenditures was greater than that for the expense companies, thus making the deferral method more useful in achieving a "smoothed" earnings stream.

4. As noted in Chapter VII, the FASB implicitly accepted the consequence of greater volatility but rejected this as an argument against FAS 2 on the basis of user needs.

5. It should be noted that some changes in R & D expenditure data for our sample may have been nominal rather than real due to discretionary changes in definition. For two reasons, however, definitional changes are not expected to be significant. First, such changes, had they existed, would likely have led to material changes in classification of R & D resulting from FAS 2. Secondly, the survey of 131 sample firms described in Chapter VIII indicated no significant changes in classification of R & D for about 95 percent of the sample.

6. "It is our contention that this (mandated switch to successful efforts) will adversely affect investors' appraisals of these companies; this in turn will impair the companies' access to the equity capital markets. . . ." (Chalsty, J., Statement by the Managing Director, Donaldson, Lufkin and Jennette before the Department of Energy, February 21, 1978, p. 2)

7. Because the book value of equity would be influenced by whether a firm used the deferral or expense method to report R & D, it was decided to measure leverage using Debt/Sales and Debt/(Total Assets—Intangibles), rather than Debt/Equity.

8. Seventy-seven percent of the deferral sample and 70 percent of the expense sample were members of the machinery (SIC code 38) industries. The remainder of the samples was comprised of firms from the following two digit industries: SIC codes 28, 34, 37, 48, and 73.

9. The results described below depend upon the analyses conducted on the two Compustat samples. The selection bias that may have resulted due to data availablility on Compustat cannot be assessed and may serve to limit generali-

zations. In addition, it should be noted that reservations have arisen about the accuracy of the R & D data in the Compustat data base prior to 1974 (San Miguel, 1977).

10. If data were unavailable for the entire period, test variables were computed on the basis of shorter intervals. This was most prevalent with respect to variables relating to R & D expenditures; for the 90 firms R & D expenditures were unavailable for 58 in 1970 and for 26 in 1971.

11. Classification of the same observations which are employed to generate the discriminant function tends to bias the misclassification rate downward. For this reason, classification accuracy also is reported below for a second (hold-out) sample.

12. Correlation among explanatory variables often creates unstable individual parameter estimates and reduces the ability to correctly measure the effect of individual variables.

Chapter XI

Summary and Implications
of Results

During the 1970s there was a significant increase in the promulgation of new standards for measuring and disclosing financial activity by public and private corporations. The purpose of this monograph has been to evaluate the justification for the increasing number of disclosure and measurement rules established by policymakers and to examine whether and how such rules affect corporate decisions.

A. SUMMARY

The primary issue in financial reporting, to what extent reporting principles need to be set by authorities as opposed to being determined by market forces, remains unanswered. The central problem for the policymaker is to determine whether an observed lack of voluntary disclosure and the existence of measurement alternatives are attributable to "market failure" or to an efficient cost/benefit evaluation by the market.

The history of the regulation of financial reporting (Chapter II) reveals that even a general framework of analysis is lacking. "Market failure" is occasionally asserted, but without any clear or verifiable meaning. Cost/benefit analysis is increasingly invoked by policymakers, but without a consistent framework of analysis. Regulatory bodies hold hearings, but without a clear method of summarizing and weighing the support for and objections to those disclosure or measurement rules under consideration. What is required is greater reliance on economic analysis to evaluate social costs and benefits, particularly when these are expected to deviate from private costs and benefits.

As described in Chapter II, the history of the regulation of financial reporting by the SEC, growing out of the Great Depression, shows that the rationale for mandated disclosure and measurement has been the perceived need to protect the investor. Protection has been sought through increased disclosure and through single, uniform measurement rules. A 1975 amendment to the Securities Act, however, has required the SEC to examine more broadly the economic effects of its own requirements. Nevertheless, it does not appear that there has been a systematic application of this requirement to financial reporting rules. The single exception, the impact of disclosure requirements on small business, was discussed in Chapter III.

Similarly, the FASB, delegated by the SEC to establish financial reporting rules subject to its oversight, has placed increased emphasis on the need to examine their cost effectiveness. Yet, in two instances discussed at length in this monograph, segment reporting (Chapter V) and the measurement of R & D investments (Chapter VII–IX), it is not clear that the Board established an effective set of criteria to evaluate its rules. In particular, the justification by the FASB for mandating segment profit reporting was based upon its prediction that forecasted earnings of multi-segment companies would improve. However, the Board did not undertake a follow-up study to determine whether, in fact, forecasts did improve and, as discussed in Chapter V, both the direct and indirect evidence of research studies performed in this area raise serious doubts about whether anticipated benefits ensued.

For the measurement of R & D expenditures, the Board and the SEC imposed an expense-only rule for all public (and, perforce, private) companies which, as detailed in Chapter VII, affected primarily smaller firms. The imposition of this expensing requirement by the two rule-making bodies was seen as an instance, similar to several others in financial reporting, where it was felt important that the "true" nature of a firm's risk be revealed. Chapters II and III reviewed the rationale for and the trend toward uniformity of measurement rules, particularly toward expensing requirements as a means of eliminating income normalization and of portraying risk. In Chapter VII it was argued that these conditions were the rationale for mandating R & D expensing.

A significant question addressed in this monograph was whether the forced change of a measurement rule by a regulatory body, leaving taxes unchanged, may result in unintended economic consequences. The preliminary discussion in Chapter II indicated that this problem, although recognized, has not yet been settled by researchers. The discussion in Chapter VI examined this problem further, summarizing the issues and evidence with respect to the economic consequences of four measurement rules. For those cases it was shown that either no research had been performed on economic effects because it was assumed that harmful effects would follow and therefore the rules were revoked or, where the rules were not revoked, the research performed on securities' returns produced results which indicated either neutral or negative effects.

In evaluating the indirect effects of rules using security returns, as in the studies reported in Chapter VI, it is extremely difficult to identify a precise "information release" time. A singular feature of the research presented in the last four chapters of the monograph was the evaluation of the internal firm effects of a measurement rule directly, rather than indirectly via securities' returns. The subject of that evaluation was the impact of the required switch to the expensing of R & D on the level and variability of R & D expenditures themselves. The methodology, tests and the conclusion that affected firms were negatively impacted were discussed in Chapter IX.

As indicated in Chapter VI, the question of whether the expense-only rule for R & D had any economic impact appears to have been ignored by the SEC, and the FASB seems to have relied on the results of a study by the U.S. Department of Commerce. As reported in Chapter VIII, because of the weakness of that study, a detailed questionnaire was distributed to a sample of small, research-intensive firms. The results of that survey supported the negative effects observed in the empirical tests.

Finally, to provide more insight into the reasons that firms select different measurement alternatives, Chapter X described the results of univariate and multivariate tests on the differences in the characteristics between those firms which deferred R & D and those which expensed prior to the passage of the expense-only rule. The findings suggested that firms which had deferred prior to the rule were smaller, less mature, less profitable, more highly levered, more research-intensive and more dependent on external funds.

B. IMPLICATIONS

Several conclusions and implications may be drawn from the research presented in this monograph. First, in the disclosure area, the SEC in the late 1970s displayed increased concern with the disclosure costs of small business, but there has not been a systematic attempt to evaluate the need for involuntary disclosure generally. Secondly, although the drive for uniformity in measurement can be traced to the formation of the SEC, there has not been a systematic examination since then of why involuntary uniformity is necessary and how its cost effectiveness may be determined. It has been shown that not only are the general models requiring uniformity not explicit, but, on occassion, the practices of the rule-making bodies seem to be inconsistent.

For instance, the FASB has viewed uniformity of measurement as a means of eliminating income smoothing by management and thus has tended to favor the selection of methods which more closely reflect a cash basis. Yet, a former official of the Commission, a leading activist, has stated that the standard-setters themselves must engage in smoothing because investors tend to be short-run. Also, the Chairman of the SEC has charged business managers with focusing too strongly on the short-run and, in this way, being partly responsible for the relative decline in U.S. productivity. Yet, no systematic effort has been made by the rule-making authorities to determine whether there is a relationship between the adoption by the Board of uniform measurement methods which increase income volatility and the alleged emphasis by management on the short-run.

In general, the research presented in this monograph points to the fact that mandated uniformity has net costs. For some financial reporting rules no benefits appear to have resulted, as the research generally indicated was the case for segment reporting. For other rules, economic costs appear to have been ignored as the research suggested was the case for the R & D expense-only rule.

Although the optimal mix of market forces and regulation has not been prescribed, what has been shown is that there has not been sufficient attention devoted to the evaluation of benefits, and that significant costs including disincentives for productivity and innovation may have been overlooked. Thus, it is suggested that rule-making bodies should perform a more thorough analysis of anticipated costs and benefits for regulations proposed in the future.

Toward this end, it would be useful to more fully understand why firms choose different measurement or disclosure rules when they are free to do so. With this knowledge, perhaps policymakers can more effectively assess the effects of their decisions on the productive sector of the economy. In addition, further investigations of the reasons which have been hypothesized for possible adverse consequences are warranted in order that they be fully understood by market participants and regulators. In sum, the evidence presented in this monograph suggests that, in considering proposed changes of financial reporting rules, regulators need to be more explicit about the alleged benefits of mandated uniformity, and need to devote more resources to the evaluation of possible adverse economic effects.

References

Chapter II

American Institute of Accountants, *Audits of Corporate Reports*. New York: AIA, 1934.

Beaver, W., "What Should Be the FASB's Objectives?" *Journal of Accountancy* (August): 49–56, 1973.

Benston, G., *Corporate Financial Disclosure in the UK and the USA*. Lexington, Mass.: Heath & Co., 1976.

Bradley, E., "Auditor's Liability and the Need for Increased Accounting Uniformity." *Law and Contemporary Problems* (Autumn): 888–922, 1965.

Burton, J., "The SEC and Financial Reporting: The Sand in the Oyster." In A. Abdel-kalik (ed.), *Government Regulation of Accounting and Information*. Gainesville: University of Florida Press, 1980.

Financial Accounting Standards Board, FAS 21, *Suspension of Reporting of Earnings Per Share and Segment Information by Nonpublic Enterprises*. Stamford, Conn.: FASB, 1978.

Financial Accounting Standards Board, *Statement of Financial Accounting Concepts (FAC) No. 1, Objectives of Financial Reporting by Business Enterprises*. Stamford Conn.: FASB, 1978.

Financial Accounting Standards Board, *Statement of Accounting Concepts (FAC) No. 2, Qualitative Characteristics of Accounting Information*. Stamford, Conn.: FASB, 1980.

Gonedes, N., and N. Dopuch, "Capital Market Equilibrium, Information Production, and Selectivity of Accounting Techniques: Framework and Review of Empirical Work." *Supplement to Journal of Accounting Research*: 48–129, 1974.

Gordon, M., "Postulates, Principles and Research in Accounting." *Accounting Review* (April): 251–263, 1964.

Holthausen, R., "Theory and Evidence on the Effect of Bond Covenants and Management Compensation Contracts on the Choice of Accounting Techniques." Unpublished Ph.D. Dissertation, University of Rochester, 1980.

Jensen, M. and W. Meckling, "Theory of the Firm: Managerial Behavior,

Agency Costs and Ownership Structure." *Journal of Financial Economics* (October): 305–360, 1976.

Keller, T., "Uniformity versus Flexibility: A Review of the Rhetoric." *Law and Contemporary Problems* (Autumn): 637–651, 1965.

Kirk, D., "How to Keep Politics Out of Standard Setting: Making Private Sector Rule-Making Work." *Journal of Accountancy* (September): 92–94, 1978.

————, Public Hearings on FASB Statement No. 19 Before the Department of Energy, February 1978.

Leftwich, R., "Private Determination of Accounting Methods in Corporate Bond Indentures." Unpublished Ph.D. Dissertation, University of Rochester, 1980.

Lev, B., "On the Adequacy of Publicly Available Financial Information for Security Analysis." In A. R. Abdel-Khalik and T. F. Keller (eds.), *Financial Information Requirements for Security Analysis*. Durham N.C.: Duke University Press, 1976.

Nader, R., M. Green, and J. Seligman, *Taming the Giant Corporation*. New York: Norton, 1976.

Parrish, M. *Securities Regulation and the New Deal*. New Haven, Conn.: Yale University Press, 1970.

Report of the Advisory Committee on Corporate Disclosure to the Securities and Exchange Commission. House Committee on Interstate and Foreign Commerce, 95th Congress, First Session, Vol. I, Washington, D.C.: GPO, November 3, 1977.

Report of Committee on Generally Accepted Accounting Principles for Smaller and/or Closely Held Business, New York: American Institute of Certified Public Accountants, 1976.

Ronen, J., "The Dual Role of Accounting: A Financial Perspective." In J. Bicksler (ed.), *Handbook of Financial Economics*. Amsterdam: North Holland, 1979.

Ross, S., "Disclosure Regulation in Financial Markets: Implications of Modern Finance Theory and Signalling Theory." In F. Edwards (ed.), *Issues in Financial Regulation*. New York: McGraw-Hill, 1979.

Securities and Exchange Act, 15 USC, Paragraph 78 w, 23 (a)(2), 1975.

Securities and Exchange Commission, Report to Congress, *The Accounting Profession and the Commission's Oversight Role*, August 1980.

Sloan, A., Jr., *My Years With General Motors*. Garden City: Doubleday, 1964.

Solomons, D., *Divisional Performance: Measurement and Control*. New York: Financial Executives Research Foundation, 1965.

Sprouse, R., "Prospects for Progress in Financial Reporting." *Financial Analysts Journal* (September-October): 56–60, 1979.

Sunder, S., "The Limits of Information." Unpublished Manuscript, University of Chicago, 1976.

Watts, R. and J. Zimmerman, "Towards a Positive Theory of the Determination of Accounting Standards." *Accounting Review* (January): 112–134, 1978.

_____, "The Demand for and Supply of Accounting Theories: The Market for Excuses." *Accounting Review* (April): 273–305, 1979.

U.S. Department of Justice, Comments on Accounting Practices of Oil and Gas Producers, File S7–715, February 27, 1978.

Williams, H., "The First Thousand Days And Beyond." Address at the Accounting Research Center, Northwestern University, April 23, 1980.

Zeff, S., *Forging Accounting Principles in Five Countries: A History and Analysis of Trends.* Champaign Ill.: Stipes Publishing Co., 1972.

Chapter III

Burton, J., "The SEC and Financial Reporting: The Sand in the Oyster." In A. Abdel-khalik (ed.), *Government Regulation of Accounting and Information.* Gainesville: University of Florida Press, 1980.

Committee on Government Operations, Subcommittee on Reports, Accounting, and Management, *The Accounting Establishment* ("Metcalf Report"). Washington, D.C.: GPO, 1977.

Financial Accounting Standards Board, FAS 19, *Financial Accounting and Reporting by Oil and Gas Companies.* Stamford, Conn.: FASB, December 1977.

Financial Accounting Standards Board, *Statement of Accounting Concepts (FAC) No. 2, Qualitative Characteristics of Accounting Information.* Stamford, Conn.: FASB, 1980.

Joint Hearings, *Small Business and Innovation,* Select Committee on Small Business, U.S. Senate and House of Representatives, 95th Congress, Second Session, Washington, D.C.: GPO, August 9 and 10, 1978.

Karmel, R., "Regulatory Reform to Assist Small Business." Remarks to the Hennepin County Bar Association, Securities Law Section, Minneapolis Minn., April 26, 1979.

Report of Committee on Generally Accepted Accounting Principles for Smaller and/or Closely Held Business, New York: American Institute of Certified Public Accountants, 1976.

Report of the Advisory Committee on Corporate Disclosure to the Securities and Exchange Commission. House Committee on Interstate and Foreign Commerce, 95th Congress, First Session, Vol. I, Washington, D.C.: GPO, November 3, 1977.

Securities and Exchange Act, 15 USC, Paragraph 78 w, 23 (a)(2), 1975.

Sprouse, R., "Prospects for Progress in Financial Reporting." *Financial Analysts Journal* (September-October): 56–60, 1979.

Williams, H., Testimony of Chairman, SEC, Before the Senate Select Committee on Small Business, September 21, 1978.

_____, "Free Enterprise in a Free Society." Address at Southern Methodist University, February 1, 1980a.

_____, "The Challenge of the New Decade," Address at Brown University, March 17, 1980b.

————, "The Economy and the Future—The Tyranny of the Short-Run." Address, November 21, 1980c.

————, "The First Thousand Days and Beyond." Address at Northwestern University, April 23, 1980d.

Chapter IV

An Analysis of Venture Capital Market Imperfections, National Bureau of Standards, Boston, Mass.: Charles River Associates, 1976.

Beaver, W., "What Should Be the FASB's Objectives." *Journal of Accountancy* (August): 49–56, 1973.

Cole, R. and P. Tegeler, *Government Requirements of Small Business.* Lexington, Mass.: Lexington Books, 1980.

Collins, D., D. Dhaliwal, and M. Rozeff, "Agency Costs, Capital Structure and Market Reaction to Nondiscretionary Accounting Changes." Working Paper, University of Iowa, 1979.

Fama, E., "Agency Problems and the Theory of the Firm." *Journal of Political Economy* (April): 288–307, 1980.

Financial Accounting Standards Board, Statement No. 7, *Accounting and Reporting by Development Stage Enterprises.* Stamford, Conn.: FASB, 1975.

Financial Analysts Federation, *Corporate Information Committee Report* (January): 11–19 and Appendix B, 1977.

Fogelson, J., "The Impact of Changes in Accounting Principles on Restrictive Covenants in Credit Agreements and Indentures." *Business Lawyer*: 769–787, 1978.

Ijiri, Y., R. Jaedicke, and K. Knight, "The Effects of Accounting Alternatives on Management Decisions." Pp. 186–199 in R. Jaedicke, et al. (eds.), *Research in Accounting Measurements.* Evanston, Ill.: American Accounting Association, 1966.

Jensen, M. C., "Some Anomalous Evidence Regarding Market Efficiency." *Journal of Financial Economics* (June): 95–101, 1978.

Jensen, M. and M. Meckling, "Theory of the Firm: Managerial Behavior, Agency Costs and Ownership Structure." *Journal of Financial Economics* (October): 305–360, 1976.

Leftwich, R., "Private Determination of Accounting Methods in Corporate Bond Indentures." Unpublished Ph.D. Dissertation, University of Rochester, 1980.

Report of the Advisory Committee on Corporate Disclosure to the Securities and Exchange Commission, House Committee on Interstate and Foreign Commerce, 95th Congress, 1st Session, Washington, D.C.: GPO.

Chapter V

Advisory Committee on Corporate Disclosure to the Securities and Exchange Commission, House Committee on Interstate and Foreign Commerce Washington, D.C.: GPO, 1977.

Arthur Andersen & Co., *Executive News Briefs* (June 7): 4, 1979.

———, *Segment Information, Disclosure of Segment Information in 1977 Annual Reports*, 1978.

Ball, R. and P. Brown, "An Empirical Evaluation of Accounting Income Numbers." *Journal of Accounting Research* (Autumn): 159–178, 1968.

———, "Portfolio Theory and Accounting." *Journal of Accounting Research* (Autumn): 300–323, 1969.

Barefield, R. and E. Comiskey, "The Impact of the SEC's Line of Business Disclosure Requirement on the Accuracy of Analysts' Forecasts of Earnings Per Share." Purdue University Working Paper, March 1975.

———, "Segmental Financial Disclosure by Diversified Firms and Security Prices: A Comment." *Accounting Review* (October): 818–821, 1975a.

Barefield, R., E. Comiskey, and A. Snyir, "Line of Business Reporting: Its Impact on Analysts' Forecasts of Earnings." Unpublished Manuscript, 1979.

Barnea, A. and J. Lakonishok, "An Analysis of the Usefulness of Disaggregated Accounting Data for Forecasts of Corporate Performance." *Decision Sciences* (January): 17–26, 1980.

Beaver, W. H. and R. E. Dukes, "Interperiod Tax Allocation, Earnings Expectations and the Behavior of Security Prices. *Accounting Review* (April): 320–332, 1972.

Burton, J., "An Interview with John C. Burton." *Management Accounting* (May): 21, 1975.

Collins, D. W., "Predicting Earnings with Subentity Data: Some Further Evidence." *Journal of Accounting Research* (Spring): 163–177, 1976.

———, SEC Line-of-Business Reporting and Earnings Forecasts." *Journal of Business Research* (May): 117–130, 1976a.

———, "SEC Product-Line Reporting and Market Efficiency." *Journal of Financial Economics* (June): 125–164, 1975.

Collins, D., and W. Dent, "The Proposed Elimination of Full Cost Accounting in the Extractive Petroleum Industry: An Empirical Assessment of Market Consequences." *Journal of Accounting and Economics*, (March): 3–44, 1979.

Collins, D. W. and R. R. Simonds, "SEC Line of Business Disclosure and Market Risk Adjustments." *Journal of Accounting Research* (Autumn): 352–383, 1979.

Corporate Financial Reporting: The Issues, the Objectives and Some New Proposals. Chicago, Ill.: CCH, 1972, pp. 67–70.

Dhaliwal, D. S., "The Impact of Disclosure Regulations on the Cost of Capital." *Conference on the Economic Consequences of Financial Accounting Standards,* Stamford, Conn.: Financial Accounting Standards Board, 1978.

Discussion Memorandum, *Reported Earnings.* Stamford, Conn.: Financial Accounting Standards Board, 1979, p. 27.

Ernst & Ernst, *Segment Reporting, A Survey of 1977 Annual Reports,* August 1978.

Exposure Draft, *Qualitative Characteristics: Criteria for Selecting and Evaluating*

Financial Accounting and Reporting Policies. Stamford, Conn.: Financial Accounting Standards Board, 1979, p. 50.

Fama, E. and M. Miller, *The Theory of Finance.* New York: Holt, Rinehart and Winston, 1972.

Financial Accounting Standards Board, Statement No. 14, *Financial Reporting for Segments of a Business Enterprise.* Stamford, Conn.: FASB, 1976.

Financial Analysts Federation, *Evaluation of Corporate Financial Reporting in Selected Industries for 1971.* New York: Financial Analysts Federation, 1972.

Foster, G., *Financial Statement Analysis.* Englewood Cliffs, N. J.: Prentice-Hall, 1978.

Goldwasser, D., "Reporting for Segments of a Business Enterprise." *Business Lawyer* (July): 2481–2490, 1978.

Griffin, P. A. and G. G. Nichols, "Segmental Disclosure Rules: An Empirical Evaluation." Unpublished Manuscript, Stanford University, June 1976.

Grunfeld, Y. and Z. Griliches, "Is Aggregation Necessarily Bad?" *Review of Economics and Statistics* (February): 1–13, 1960.

Handbook on the EEC Fourth Directive. New York: Price Waterhouse & Co., 1979.

Hessen, R., *In Defense of the Corporation.* Stanford, Ca.: Hoover Institution Press, 1979.

Horwitz, B. and R. Kolodny, "Line of Business Reporting and Security Prices: An Analysis of an SEC Disclosure Rule." *Bell Journal of Economics* (Spring): 234–249, 1977.

————, "Line of Business Reporting: A Rejoinder." *Bell Journal of Economics* (Autumn): 659–663, 1978.

Kinney, W. R., Jr., "Predicting Earnings: Entity versus Subentity Data." *Journal of Accounting Research* (Spring): 127–136, 1971.

Kochanek, R., "Segmental Financial Disclosure and Security Prices." *Accounting Review* (April): 245–258, 1974.

————, "Segmental Financial Disclosure by Diversified Firms and Security Prices: A Reply." *Accounting Review* (October): 822–825, 1975.

Lintner, J., "The Valuation of Risk Assets and the Selection of Risky Investments in Stock Portfolios and Capital Budgets." *Review of Economics and Statistics* (February): 13–37, 1965.

Mautz, R., *Financial Reporting by Diversified Companies.* New York: Financial Executives Institute, 1968.

McNamar, R., "FTC Line-of-Business Reporting: Fact and Fiction." *Financial Executive* (August): 20–27, 1974.

Mossin, J., "Equilibrium in a Capital Asset Market." *Econometrica* (October): 768–783, 1966.

Plum, C. and D. Collins, "Business Segment Reporting." In Edwards, J. and R. Wixon (eds), *Modern Accountant's Handbook.* Homewood, Ill.: Dow Jones-Irwin, 1976.

Rappaport, A. and E. Lerner, *A Framework for Financial Reporting by Diversified Companies.* New York: National Association of Accountants, 1969.

Rubinstein, M., "A Mean-Variance Synthesis of Corporate Financial Theory." *Journal of Finance* (March): 167–181, 1973.

Scherer, F. M., "Statistics for Government Regulation." *American Statistician* (February): 1–5, 1979.

Schiff, M., "A Note on Transfer Pricing and Industry Segment Reporting." *Journal of Accounting, Auditing, and Finance* (Spring): 224–231, 1979.

Sharpe, W. F., "Capital Asset Prices: A Theory of Market Equilibrium Under Conditions of Risk." *Journal of Finance* (September): 425–442, 1964.

Simonds, R. R. and D. W. Collins, "Line of Business Reporting and Security Prices: An Analysis of an SEC Disclosure Rule: Comment." *Bell Journal of Economics* (Autumn):646–658, 1978.

Sommer, A. A., Jr., "Financial Reporting and the Stock Market: The Other Side of the Issue." *Financial Executive* (May): 36–40, 1974.

Sprouse, R., "Prospects for Progress in Financial Reporting." *Financial Analysts Journal* (September-October): 56–60, 1979.

Statement on Auditing Standards No. 21 (Segment Reporting). New York: American Institute of Certified Public Accountants, December 1977.

Tuck, C., "The Impact of Disclosure Regulations on the Cost of Capital: Comment." *Conference on the Economic Consequences of Financial Accounting Standards*. Stamford, Conn.: Financial Accounting Standards Board, 1978.

Twombly, J., "Historical Origins of Segment Reporting." Unpublished Manuscript, Northwestern University, 1977.

———, "Segment Reporting." Unpublished Manuscript, Northwestern University, 1978.

Wheat Report, *Disclosure to Investors*. Chicago Ill.: CCH, Inc., 1969.

Chapter VI

Accounting Principles Board, *Accounting for the "Investment Credit"*, APB 2. New York: AICPA, 1962.

Accounting Principles Board, *Accounting for the "Investment Credit"*, APB 4. New York: AICPA, 1964.

Chalsty, J., Statement by Managing Director, Donaldson, Lufkin & Jennette at the Department of Energy Hearings, February 21, 1978, p. 2.

Collins, D. and W. Dent, "The Proposed Elimination of Full Cost Accounting in the Extractive Petroleum Industry: An Empirical Assessment of the Market Consequences." *Journal of Accounting and Economics* (March): 3–44, 1979.

Commons, D., Outline of Presentation at the Department of Energy Hearings, undated.

Department of the Treasury, Letter to Senator R. Long from C. E. Walker, Acting Secretary, November 12, 1971.

Department of the Treasury, Statement of Deputy Assistant Secretary (Tax Analysis), E. M. Sunley, Before the Oversight Subcommittee of the Committee on Ways and Means, March 28, 1979.

Dyckman, T. and A. Smith, "Financial Accounting and Reporting by Oil and Gas Producing Companies: A Study of Information Effects." *Journal of Accounting and Economics* (March): 45–75, 1979.

Ernst & Ernst, Letter to the Financial Accounting Standards Board on the Exposure Draft for FAS 2, August 2, 1974.

Federal Trade Commission, Bureau of Competition, Comments Before the SEC Concerning Accounting Practices of Oil and Gas Producers, File S7–715, May 1978, p. 7.

Financial Accounting Standards Board, *Accounting for Contingencies*, Statement No. 5. Stamford, Conn.: FASB, 1975.

Financial Accounting Standards Board, *Accounting and Reporting By Development Stage Enterprises*, Statement No. 7. Stamford, Conn.: FASB, 1975.

Financial Accounting Standards Board, *Accounting for the Translation of Foreign Currency Transactions and Foreign Currency Financial Statements*, Statement No. 8. Stamford, Conn.: FASB, 1975.

Financial Accounting Standards Board, *Financial Accounting and Reporting By Oil and Gas Producing Companies*, Statement No. 19. Stamford, Conn.: FASB, 1977.

Kirk, D., Address to the Annual Conference of the National Association of Accountants, January 23, 1978.

Securities and Exchange Act, 15 USC, Paragraph 78 w(a)(2), June 4, 1975.

Securities and Exchange Commission, *Accounting for the "Investment Credit"*, Accounting Series Release 96, Chicago: CCH, Inc., 1963.

Shank, J., J. Dillard, and R. Murdock, *Assessing the Impact of FASB No. 8*, New York: Financial Executive Research Foundation, 1979.

U.S. Department of Commerce, "Impact of FASB's Rule Two Accounting for Research and Development Costs on Small/Developing Stage Firms." Washington, D.C.: U.S. Department of Commerce, Domestic Business Policy Analysis Staff, January 20, 1975.

Chapter VII

Barron's, "The FASB Goes to Work." P. 3, November 18, 1974.

Business Week, "Vanishing Innovation. Pp. 46–54, July 3, 1978.

Coopers & Lybrand, Letter to FASB on Statements 1–12, August 1978.

Federal Trade Commission, Bureau of Competition, Comments Before the SEC Concerning Accounting Practices of Oil and Gas Producers, File S7–715, May 1978, p. 7.

Financial Accounting Standards Board, Statement No. 2, *Accounting for Research and Development Costs*. Stamford, Conn.: FASB, October 1974.

Financial Accounting Standards Board, Public Record, Volume XI, Position Papers on Exposure Draft for FAS 2, December 31, 1974.

Financial Accounting Standards Board, Statement No. 25, *Suspension of Certain Accounting Requirements for Oil and Gas Producing Companies*, Stamford, Conn.: FASB, 1979.

Gellein, O. and M. Newman, *Accounting for Research and Development Expendi-*

tures. New York: American Institute of Certified Public Accountants, 1973.

Jewkes, J., et al., *The Sources of Invention,* 2nd Edition. New York: Norton, 1969.

Joint Hearings Before the Select Committee on Small Business, U.S. Senate and the Committee on Small Business, House of Representatives, *Small Business and Innovation,* 95th Congress, 2nd Session, Washington, D.C.: GPO, 1978.

Kamien, M. and N. Schwartz, "Market Structure and Innovation: A Survey." *Journal of Economic Literature* (March): 1–37, 1975.

Mansfield, E., et al., Pp. 170–172 in *Research and Innovation in the Modern Corporation.* New York: Norton, 1971.

Orton, B. and R. Bradish, "Accounting for R & D." *Management Accounting* (July): 31–42, 1969.

Peck, M. J., "Inventions in the Post-War American Aluminum Industry." Pp. 279–292 in *The Rate and Direction of Inventive Activity: Economic and Social Factors.* Princeton, N.J.: National Bureau of Economic Research, 1962.

San Miguel, J., "Accounting by Business Firms for Investment in Research and Development." Unpublished Manuscript, New York University, August 1975.

Sprouse, R., "Prospects for Progress in Financial Reporting." *Financial Analysts Journal* (September-October): 56–60, 1979.

Williams, H., "Financial Reporting In A Changing Economic Environment." New York: May 31, 1979.

Yankelovich, Skelly and White, Inc., *A Business Perspective on Technological Innovation.* New York, August 1980.

Chapter VIII

Disclosure Journal: Index of Corporate Events, Volume III (May 1974–April 1975).

Exposure Draft, Financial Accounting Standards Board, "Qualitative Characteristics: Criteria for Selecting and Evaluating Financial Accounting and Reporting Policies," August 1979.

Financial Accounting Standards Board, Statement No. 2, *Accounting for Research and Development Costs.* Stamford, Conn.: FASB, October 1974.

Financial Executives Institute, Letter to the FASB, File Reference No. 1007, March 11, 1974.

Hollander, M. and D. Wolfe, *Nonparametrical Statistical Methods.* New York: Wiley, 1973.

Mosaic, Volume 10, Number 2, Washington, D.C.: National Science Foundation, March/April 1979, p. 46.

Recommendations for Creating Jobs Through the Success of Small, Innovative Business, A Report of the Commerce Technical Advisory Board to Jordan J. Baruch, Assistant Secretary for Science and Technology, U.S. Department of Commerce, December 1978.

Report of the Advisory Committee on Corporate Disclosure to the Securities and Exchange Commission, House Committee on Interstate and Foreign Commerce, Vol. I, Washington, D.C.: GPO, 1977.

Chapter X

Bierman, H. and R. Dukes, "Accounting for Research and Development Costs." *Journal of Accountancy* (April): 48–55, 1975.

Burton, J. C., "Conflicts and Compromises in Financial Reporting." Stanford Lectures in Accounting, 1976.

Deakin III, E. B. "An Analysis of Differences Between Nonmajor Oil Firms Using Successful Efforts and Full Cost Methods." *Accounting Review* (October): 722–734, 1979.

Dhaliwal, D., "The Effects of the Firm's Capital Structure on the Choice of Accounting Methods." *Accounting Review* (January): 78–84, 1980.

Financial Accounting Standards Board, Statement No. 2, *Accounting for Research and Development Costs.* Stamford, Conn.: FASB, October 1974.

Financial Accounting Standards Board, Statement No. 19, *Accounting for Reporting by Oil and Gas Producing Companies.* Stamford, Conn.: FASB, 1977.

Gellein, O. and M. Newman, *Accounting for Research and Development Expenditures,* Research Study No. 14. New York: AICPA, 1973.

Gordon, M., "Postulates, Principles and Research in Accounting." *Accounting Review* (April): 44–62, 1964.

Hagerman, R. L. and M. E. Zmijewski, "Some Economic Determinants of Accounting Policy Choice." *Journal of Accounting and Economics* (October): 141–166, 1979.

San Miguel, J., "Accounting by Business Firms for Investment in Research and Development." Unpublished Manuscript, New York University, August 1975.

———, "The Relationship of R & D Data in COMPUSTAT and 10-K Reports." *Accounting Review* (July): 638–641, 1977.

Sorter, G., et al., "Accounting and Financial Measures as Indicators of Corporate Personality—Some Empirical Findings." In R. Jaedicke, et al. (eds.), *Research in Accounting Measurement.* Evanston, Ill.: American Accounting Association, 1966.

United States Department of Justice, "Comments on Accounting Practices—Oil and Gas Producers—Financial Accounting Standards." Before the Securities and Exchange Commission, February 27, 1978.

Watts, R. and J. Zimmerman, "Towards a Positive Theory of the Determination of Accounting Standards." *Accounting Review* (January): 112–134, 1978.

Acknowledgments

The following chapters contain reprinted material from the various journals indicated.

Chapter IV

"The Economic Effects of Involuntary Uniformity in the Financial Reporting of R & D Expenditures," vol. 18, Supplement, copyright © 1980 by the *Journal of Accounting Research*. Reprinted with permission.
"The FASB, and SEC and R & D," vol. 12, copyright © 1981 (Spring) by the *Bell Journal of Economics*. Reprinted with permission.

Chapter V

"Segment Reporting: Hindsight After Ten Years," vol. 4, no. 1, copyright © 1980 (Fall) by the *Journal of Accounting, Auditing and Finance*. Reprinted with permission.

Chapter VII

"The Economic Effects of Involuntary Uniformity in the Financial Reporting of R & D Expenditures," vol. 18, Supplement, copyright © 1980 by the *Journal of Account Research*. Reprinted with permission.
"Financial Reporting Regulation and Small Research-Intensive Firms," copyright © 1982 by the *Journal of Small Business Management*. Reprinted with permission.

Chapter VIII

Chapter IX

Chapter X

Author Index

Subject Index